The Rebel in his Family
Selected Papers of William Smith O'Brien

IRISH NARRATIVES

IRISH NARRATIVES

Series edited by David Fitzpatrick

Personal narratives of past lives are essential for understanding any field of history. They provide unrivalled insight into the day-to-day consequences of political, social, economic or cultural relationships. Memoirs, diaries and personal letters, whether by public figures or obscure witnesses of historical events, will often captivate the general reader as well as engrossing the specialist. Yet the vast majority of such narratives are preserved only among the manuscripts or rarities in libraries and archives scattered over the globe. The aim of this series of brief yet scholarly editions is to make available a wide range of narratives concerning Ireland and the Irish over the last four centuries. All documents, or sets of documents, are edited and introduced by specialist scholars, who guide the reader through the world in which the text was created. The chosen texts are faithfully transcribed, the biographical and local background explored, and the documents set in historical context. This series will prove invaluable for university and school teachers, providing superb material for essays and textual analysis in class. Above all, it offers a novel opportunity for readers interested in Irish history to discover fresh and exciting sources of personal testimony.

Other titles in the series:

Andrew Bryson's Ordeal: An Epilogue to the 1798 Rebellion, edited by Michael Durey
Henry Stratford Persse's Letters from Galway to America, 1821–1832, edited by James L. Pethica and James C. Roy
A Redemptorist Missionary in Ireland, 1851–1854: Memoirs by Joseph Prost, translated and edited by Emmet Larkin and Herman Freudenberger
Frank Henderson's Easter Rising, edited by Michael Hopkinson
A Patriot Priest: The Life of Father James Coigly, 1761–1798, edited by Dáire Keogh
'My Darling Danny': Letters from Mary O'Connell to her son Daniel, 1830–1832, edited by Erin I. Bishop

Forthcoming titles:

The Reynolds Letters: An Irish Emigrant Family in Late Victorian Manchester, edited by Lawrence W. McBride
A Policeman's Ireland: Recollections of Samuel Waters, RIC, edited by Stephen Ball

David Fitzpatrick teaches history at Trinity College, Dublin. His books include *Politics and Irish Life, 1913–1921* (1977, reissued 1998) and *Oceans of Consolation: Personal Accounts of Irish Migration to Australia* (1995).

The Rebel in his Family
Selected Papers of William Smith O'Brien

Edited by
Richard and Marianne Davis

CORK UNIVERSITY PRESS

First published in 1998 by
Cork University Press
Cork
Ireland

British Library Cataloguing in Publication Data

A CIP catalogue record for this book is available from the British Library.

ISBN 1 85918 181 3

Typesetting by Red Barn Publishing, Skeagh, Skibbereen

Printed in Ireland by ColourBooks, Baldoyle, Co. Dublin

Contents

Acknowledgements

We are indebted to the Australian Research Council for grants to work on the William Smith O'Brien Papers. The National Library of Ireland gave access to the original manuscripts, available normally only on microfilm. Mr Anthony O'Brien of Dublin made available his considerable collection of his ancestor's correspondence and memorabilia. Likewise Dr Robin Gwynn, formerly of Massey University, Palmerston North, New Zealand, and now of Napier, New Zealand, gave access to his valuable family letters. Research assistance was provided by Mrs Susan Johnson, Mrs Lyn Rainbird, Mrs Heather Banks, Mrs Kate Walpole, Mrs Andrea Gerrard, Mr Tim Jetson, Dr Simon Harris and Mrs Cherrill Vertigan.

Introduction

Unlike Irish revolutionary leaders such as Theobald Wolfe Tone, Robert Emmet, John Mitchel, Jeremiah O'Donovan Rossa and Pádraic Pearse, William Smith O'Brien has never aroused much enthusiasm. No full biography has been published before 1998. His idealism is acknowledged, but his personality appears stiff, arrogant and unapproachable. Yet his life was dramatic. Born in 1803 as the second son in a family which combined the ancient Gaelic tradition of King Brian Boru with the ascendancy of the nineteenth-century Irish Protestant landed establishment, O'Brien had every worldly advantage. An English education at Harrow, private establishments, Trinity College, Cambridge, and Lincoln's Inn was capped in 1828 when he was nominated by his father, Sir Edward O'Brien, Bart, of Dromoland, to the rotten borough of Ennis, county town of Clare.

Though forced to relinquish Ennis in 1831 to another aristocratic potentate, O'Brien had the good luck to inherit, through his mother, his grandfather William Smith's property of Cahirmoyle in County Limerick. This enabled him to secure election in 1835 as one of the two members for that county. From 1835 to 1843 O'Brien held the seat as an independent radical, supportive of the Act of Union, but industrious in parliament for Irish reform. He kept aloof from Daniel O'Connell, whose victory in the Clare election of 1828 not only brought about Catholic Emancipation but undermined the traditional political influence of the O'Brien family there. However, to the consternation of his family, in late 1843 O'Brien joined O'Connell's Repeal Association. He became an alternative leader of the organisation. The Young Ireland ginger group, led by Thomas Davis and Charles Gavan Duffy, associated with the *Nation* newspaper, supported him. A split with O'Connell took place in 1846, and O'Brien and the Young Irelanders formed a rival organisation, the Irish Confederation, also pledged to secure Irish self-government.

The British government's inability to relieve the Great Famine of 1845–49 was bitterly denounced by O'Brien in parliament. Stimulated by the 1848 revolutions in Europe, O'Brien was persuaded to lead an ill-organised rising in Tipperary in July of that year. Condemned to be hanged, drawn and quartered for treason, O'Brien and his chief lieutenants were reprieved and transported for life to Van Diemen's Land in July 1849. But a conditional pardon arrived in 1854, and O'Brien lived in Europe until a full pardon was conceded in 1856. Returning home as a martyred hero, O'Brien refused to re-enter parliament or contemplate a further rising. He retained his belief in the righteousness of his cause, and was recognised as an elder statesman. He published frequent addresses to the Irish people before his death in 1864.

The bare bones of the William Smith O'Brien story are relatively well known. For an aristocrat raised in Dromoland Castle, now a luxury hotel, to be reduced to a tiny cottage in the penal station for secondary offenders at Port Arthur appeals to romantic imagination. But William Smith O'Brien was neither a romantic nor a vague idealist. His massive collection of political and private papers portrays a well-rounded, if querulous, individual. In 1995 O'Brien's journal of exile in Van Diemen's Land was belatedly published. Apart from his seventeen active years in the House of Commons, his nationalist politics and his four and a half years of political exile in Tasmania, O'Brien was an enthusiastic traveller through Europe, North America, Australia and even India, producing a number of journals of his expeditions. Political, social and economic historians mine the William Smith O'Brien Papers, supplemented by the Inchiquin Papers of the wider family.

The student of Smith O'Brien discovers, behind the parliamentarian, the nationalist agitator and rebel, the dismal but active penal exile and the inveterate traveller, the power of O'Brien family solidarity. Though frequently in total disagreement with his nearest and dearest relations, Smith O'Brien never experienced abandonment or separation. The O'Brien clan demonstrated a pragmatic adaptability to circumstances which enabled it to retain territory dating back to the great King Brian Boru in the eleventh century. The house of Dromoland, originally a junior branch of the royal O'Briens, was rewarded with a baronetcy in the seventeenth century. It became the senior branch when Smith O'Brien's brother Lucius in 1862 achieved recognition as the thirteenth Baron Inchiquin. In the eighteenth century, however, the Dromoland baronets played a leading role in the all-Protestant Irish parliament and were well known as improving farmers, smuggling some wine on the side. Smith O'Brien's father, Sir Edward, voted against the Act of Union, but nevertheless took his seat in the united parliament at Westminster.

Political activity was costly in the early nineteenth century. Free-holders, in fact the tenants of the local landlords, were brought, with expenses paid, to the county town to vote. MPs received no salaries. Irish members had to travel to Westminster, a long and tedious journey by coach and boat, taking two to three days, and hire accommodation in London during sessions which absorbed a greater part of the year. Meanwhile their estates in Ireland needed efficient spouses or reliable bailiffs. Not surprisingly, a number of Irish landlords lived permanently in England or, when members of parliament, cut short their attendance at sessions. Despite his large estate, Sir Edward found himself in debt and had to engage the services of a self-made attorney, William Smith, whose fortune was apparently derived from buying up and trafficking in the mortgages of indebted landowners. Smith advised Sir Edward to marry one of his two daughters and heirs. Sir Edward complied. Although his bluff patriarchal religious tolerance ill agreed with his wife's parvenu evangelical endeavours to convert her husband's Catholic tenantry to Protestantism, the marriage was happy.

The heir to Sir Edward's title and Dromoland estate, Lucius (1800–72), was first of a family of thirteen. A sister, Grace (1802–71), destined to remain unmarried, was followed in October 1803 by the second son, William (1803–64). His grandfather William Smith made a complicated will. His legitimate daughters Charlotte and Harriet obtained a life interest in his property independent of their husbands. After Charlotte the residue of her estate went first to William, who subsequently added Smith to his name. Smith's children by a mistress, Brigit Keevan, also had some reversionary rights.

This was to cause problems when an imposter, John V. Crosbie, with the support of Smith's daughter Jane, claimed to be the long-dead Thomas Smith [19, 20].[1] Other children of Sir Edward and Lady O'Brien were Edward (1806–40), Robert (1809–70), Henry (1813–95), Anne (1805–72), Harriet (1812–83) and Catherine (Kate) (1817–65). Edward practised as a London lawyer; Robert acted as estate manager for his brothers; Henry became a Church of Ireland parson. Anne and Grace, close to their brother William, were frequent correspondents in later life, Anne marrying the Rev. Arthur Martineau and living at Whitkirk Vicarage, Yorkshire. Harriet married the Rev. Charles Monsell, brother of a rival parliamentarian in County Limerick, and Catherine the Rev. Charles Harris, later Bishop of Gibraltar. There was less correspondence between William and his younger sisters. Lady O'Brien, responsible for a large family, outlived her husband by nearly twenty years, dying at the age of seventy-five in 1856.

In his boyhood years William O'Brien was devoted to his elder brother Lucius. He did not enjoy his childhood, complaining later that in his day 'it was supposed that a boy who suffered hardships vexations and tyranny in his youth' could more easily cope with later difficulties and disappointments. At the age of four his father found him 'as quick and intelligent as any boy I ever saw of his age and forwarder at his books than most boys of six or seven'.[2] There was little time for childhood. As with many sons of the gentry, he was sent, apparently at the age of six, to boarding school, in his case in Kent. This meant a long separation from family. As a Westminster MP Sir Edward monitored his children at school in England. In 1812, when William was nine, Sir Edward was concerned about an undisclosed complaint, requiring medical investigation. This may have been related to the deafness which ran in the family. In the following year William and his brother Lucius went together to Harrow. They remained at Harrow for three years. William's attendance at Harrow when aged only nine is paralleled by his parliamentary contemporary, the Whig Prime Minister Lord Melbourne, who entered Eton equally young.

We have no description of William at Harrow, apart from his placement in the fourth form and his later assertion that he secured a good grounding there in the classics. At the age of fifteen we find him a student of the Rev. Berry Scott's establishment at Harborough Magna, near Rugby. As a younger son he was required to choose a profession from a limited list of army, navy, law or the church. William was early attracted to the navy, but James O'Brien's response in February 1819 to a request for advice deterred him [1]. James, of Woodfield, County Clare, a cousin of William's father, had been brought up with the latter and took a keen interest in Sir Edward's children.[3] As an army lieutenant James may have had a natural bias against the navy, but reviewed current prospects in economic terms, with only a slight whiff of idealism. Hinting at personal disappointment, James ruled out both army and navy, suitable for those of 'inferior talents', lacking steadiness and destitute of fortune or friends. The law, though dry, would suit young William's 'pleasure in study', and combined with parliament could satisfy ambition. The church was not mentioned.

William's letter to his mother in March, announcing that he had given up any idea of the navy, rehearsed his cousin's arguments [2]. He also introduced a strong note of piety, absent in James O'Brien's advice, and saw the hand of God in his decision. This evangelical spirit pervades many of William's letters of this time. In another letter, written a few days later, he talked at length of sin and temptation and the need for his mother's prayers: 'I know very well that I might as well trust to a broken reed as to myself and without God's assistance I could not resist temptation.'[4] We see here the strong influence of his mother, whose own correspondence often contained lengthy evangelical exhortation. We also perceive William as a rather sad, almost neglected, boy, uncertain of his reception in the holidays and longing for a little privacy in Scott's establishment. He conscientiously asked for books to pursue the literary path his elders have mapped out for him. William's letter to his mother in September 1819 shows that he had either internalised the latter's evangelical teaching and become priggishly conscientious or, less likely, has adopted the style to please his mother [3]. The Rev. Mr

Scott's fishing was unacceptable to young William. The schoolboy considered hunting to be associated with unrefined company. He believed exercise essential and worried whether he took enough for a growing boy. Nor did he forget the needs of the Dromoland poor. Two years later William addressed another serious letter to his parents. He now accepted their long-expressed desire that he should study for the bar, 'as the most extensive sphere of usefulness, and the best suited to my ambition, my hopes and my expectation'. While confessing that 'my talents are moderate', he expressed the hope that, with enthusiasm, a good education and application, he would succeed as a lawyer. Ambitious 'to serve and do good to my country; my desire is to prove myself not unworthy [of] such a father as you, nor of the honorable name of O'Brien, of that family which has always been the defender and guardian of its country'.[5]

Eventually separated from Mr Scott, whose tuition left much to be desired, William became an undergraduate at Trinity College, Cambridge, in the years 1821–26, and a law student at the King's Inns, Dublin, and Lincoln's Inn, London. His actions were no longer as conscientious as his earlier sentiments suggested. Sir Edward, considered his second son good company when they shared London accommodation in 1825, but found him too keen to mix in high society and too indolent to apply himself to arduous legal studies [4]. Kept meticulously after May 1826, William's day book chronicles a round of balls, theatres and operas in London, while in Clare billiards, hunting, shooting and fishing predominated. William grew up tall, strong and a skilled horseman. The priggish, sin-obsessed schoolboy of the Scott period disappeared. He described himself as 'toxicated' after a family celebration. His father lamented that William's 'unfortunate Cambridge affair' had put all thoughts of legal practice out of his mind. Details of the affair are lacking, but in 1826 William was a frequent visitor in London to Mrs Wilton, or 'Mrs W' as she became in the day book. Anticipating a later period, we have a letter in 1830 from his brother Lucius, paying off Mary Anne Wilton, who had just been delivered of a child [5]. This was not the end of the affair, as Mary Anne, claiming to be

Mrs O'Brien, bore another child, a daughter, whom she also attributed to him. Although there is no acknowledegment of the second child, William was certainly sowing his wild oats.

An anxious Sir Edward nominated William for the family seat of Ennis at a by-election in April 1828, less than three months before the epoch-making by-election victory of Daniel O'Connell for County Clare. William joined Lucius, already one of the two MPs for County Clare. To his father's relief and surprise, William, though still only twenty-four, responded positively to parliamentary duties, outshining Lucius. The difficult son appeared to have found a useful occupation at last. William was popular locally as one of only two MPs to be members of Daniel O'Connell's Catholic Association, dedicated to securing the right of Catholics to sit at Westminster. Unfortunately the climax of the movement, which achieved Catholic Emancipation in 1829, was Daniel O'Connell's victory in the County Clare election of July 1828, in the teeth of O'Brien family opposition. Supporting O'Brien interests, William fought two duels with O'Connell adherents. The Dromoland O'Briens saw their political influence in Clare shattered. Lucius lost his Clare seat in 1830, and William was forced to give up his Ennis seat in 1831 to O'Connell's defeated opponent of 1828, William Vesey-Fitzgerald.

Pretty Lucy Gabbett (1811–61), the daughter of Joseph Gabbett, a Protestant landowner and Tory Mayor of Limerick for 1819–20, thwarted his immediate political aspirations. Lucy and William were married in late 1832 after a short courtship. Impressed by the new stability of her second son, Lady O'Brien allowed him part of her father's Cahirmoyle estate. William remained financially dependent on his formidable mother. With his father-in-law's assistance, he threw himself into the internal affairs of Limerick, concerning himself in particular with the development of the port, emigration and the poor law. At the general election of 1835 William, with the tacit endorsement of O'Connell, whose anti-Tory party he joined, was elected for County Limerick as a radical Whig MP, forcing a sitting member to withdraw before the poll. Meanwhile his brother Lucius was humiliatingly defeated as a Tory candidate in Clare when his election partner with-drew at the last moment, compelling Lucius to retire without receiving a vote. While William remained aloof from O'Connell until 1843, his basic support came from Catholic clergy linked to the Liberator. On the other hand, as MPs were then unpaid, he needed subventions from his Tory and evangelical Protestant mother to stay in parliament.

At first William and Lucy travelled together to London for the par-liamentary sessions. This necessitated a three-day journey by boat and coach and the perennial anxiety of obtaining suitable lodgings near Westminster. As an experienced House of Commons wife, Lady O'Brien had sage advice on accommodation for parliamentary sessions which could run from January to August, warning of boredom for Lucy. She also criticised her son's attempt to secure an Irish poor law for the aged and infirm, arguing that work-shy habits and alehouses were the real problem [6]. An Irish poor law was high on William's agenda. He was fully occupied in supporting the Whig government and striving for effective Irish legislation on emigration, municipal reform and public education, as well as provision for the destitute. Lucy, mean-while, had less to do. The couple became very close to William's Cam-bridge friend, duelling second and lawyer, Woronzow Greig (1805–65) and his wife Agnes.

The birth of William's long-awaited son and heir, Edward William (Ned) (1837–1909), and the six children who followed — William Joseph (Willie) (1839–67), Lucy Josephine (1840–1907), Lucius Henry (1842–1913), Robert Donough (Don) (1844–1917), Charlotte Grace (1845–1909) and Charles Murrough (Charley) (1849–77) — transformed the pattern of O'Brien life. The first months of 1837 were a traumatic period for the family. William was engaged in bitter con-troversy with the great Daniel O'Connell; his grandfather Smith's nat-ural daughter, Jane Brew, was backing an imposter, John V. Crosbie, claiming to be Thomas Smith with rights to part of Smith O'Brien's estate; worst of all, his revered father was dying. Lady O'Brien wanted her first grandchild to be born at Dromoland Castle, but Lucy naturally preferred her mother's assistance at 78 George's Street, Limerick. Sir

Edward's dying request that the grandson be taken to him could not be met, as an influenza epidemic at Dromoland threatened the child [8, 9]. Lady O'Brien nevertheless had very clear ideas on the proper feeding of young children, which she conveyed to her daughter-in-law by letter [9].

Shortly before Sir Edward's death Lucius married Mary Fitzgerald, who now became Lady O'Brien and mistress of Dromoland Castle, reducing the formidable Charlotte to wealthy dowager status. Although the latter opted to live mainly at Dromoland, she appears at one stage to have considered Cahirmoyle, in which she still had a life interest. This, fortunately for William, did not take place. The latter's problems increased with his growing family. At first he endeavoured to take Lucy and the baby to London, but with further accouchements and the needs of the children, this became less easy. William Joseph, born deaf and thus practically dumb, was a great problem for the family. For a time he attended a special establishment in England. Many of the family suffered the same complaint to a lesser degree.

Financial problems increased apace. When he heard of Lucy's second pregnancy, William resolved to give up parliament if his mother did not provide him with another £1,000 p.a. [10]. Fortunately he was not forced to carry out his threat. However, his mother lectured him on the impossibility of gaining a living from the Cahirmoyle estate if he insisted on spending so much time at Westminster. She had obligations to her other children [11].

When Lucy was unable to accompany him to London, William expected constant correspondence and encouragement. He wrote regularly about his problems and scolded Lucy if her letters did not arrive daily, especially when London was dull in the summer [12]. This was difficult when children were sick or when other domestic crises occurred. During one child's serious illness Lucy was glad of her husband's absence: 'I spend my day in the nursery where you could be of no sort of use.'[6] When Lucy complained of the strain of perpetual pregnancies on her far from strong constitution, she was rebuked in strongly patriarchal terms by her husband [18]. But she wrote regularly to

William, often despondent when away from home. In 1844, when he was busy in Dublin, Lucy urged him to find comfortable lodgings and attend literary meetings in the evenings [17].

Such was the life of an Irish independent radical MP and his family in the 1830s and early 1840s. William's adhesion to O'Connell's Repeal Association in late 1843, long expected by political pundits, caused a family crisis. Charlotte, in two highly charged letters, denounced her son's decision and hinted at economic reprisals. Nevertheless, she took no decisive action which might have forced the errant William out of politics [14, 15]. O'Brien solidarity was not so easily shaken, and there was no rift in the family. Although O'Connell was pledged to non-violence, Charlotte, hysterically but correctly, anticipated her son's indictment for treason. William, who continued to respect his mother, tried not to quarrel with her. Only occasionally did his exasperation show through as in an exchange caused by the continued demands of Charlotte's half-sister, Jane Brew [19, 20].

Smith O'Brien's political *volte-face* led to worrying new activity. Instead of attending parliament in 1844, he travelled to Dublin to act as O'Connell's lieutenant at the weekly public meetings of his Repeal Association [16, 17, 18]. He was received with ecstatic applause when he entered the Repeal Association meeting after O'Connell's bitterly resented conviction and imprisonment for sedition. But a 'trembling' Lucy reminded William of divisions at home, where his father-in-law, Joseph Gabbett, strongly opposed O'Connell, his mother-in-law, Lucy Gabbett, secretly supported the Liberator, and his little daughter Lucy Josephine wanted to rush to her father's aid [16]. William continued to act as Repeal leader until, a few months later, the House of Lords reversed the verdict and released the Liberator.

O'Connell's gratitude to O'Brien diminished in 1845 when the latter became associated with the Repeal ginger group, sometimes known as Young Ireland. Its leader, the Protestant Thomas Davis, who died tragically in late 1845, worked closely with O'Brien. Lucy and William's sister Anne were most impressed with Davis, if not with O'Connell. After Davis's death O'Brien in 1846 followed the Repeal policy of handling only Irish business in parliament, refusing to sit on a Scottish railway committee. For his intransigence he was imprisoned for twenty-five days in the precincts of the House of Commons. O'Connell was lukewarm in O'Brien's support, but the Young Irelanders were enthusiastic. William relayed his anger against O'Connell to Lucy from his improvised jail and threatened to resign from parliament. Lucy shared her husband's annoyance at the O'Connell clique, but was preoccupied with more homely topics, such as their servant Richard's report on their unfortunate deaf son Willie, and their journey to a special school in England [22, 23, 32].

After a few weeks O'Brien was released, but relations between himself, the Young Irelanders and O'Connell's close adherents continued to deteriorate. Quarrelling over O'Connell's strong support for the new Whig government and the Repeal Association's attempt to exclude even theoretical believers in force from membership, O'Brien led the Young Irelanders out of the Repeal Association in July 1846. In early 1847 they established a rival organisation, the Irish Confederation, of which William accepted *de facto* leadership, along with Charles Gavan Duffy, editor of the influential Young Ireland newspaper, the *Nation*.

Meanwhile the disastrous potato famine had taken hold on Ireland. In speech after speech in parliament O'Brien and other Irish members denounced the failure of Lord John Russell's Whig government to provide adequate relief and their inappropriate philosophy of *laissez-faire*, generating the distribution, not of food, but of leaflets quoting Adam Smith against government action. At Dromoland the Dowager Lady O'Brien worked hard to provide relief for suffering tenants. Although she had earlier denounced the squandering of money in alehouses, she now agreed in rejecting the government's lukewarm measures for dealing with the crisis. The charity soup, devised by Soyer, was totally insufficient to provide necessary energy [24].

The revolutions throughout Europe in early 1848 and the continued rack of the famine inflamed Irish Confederation moderates such as Smith O'Brien and Gavan Duffy. They vied with the militants led by John Mitchel in using bellicose language. The Confederation sponsored

clubs, proliferating throughout the country and apparently drilling for
an insurrection. Russell's administration bided its time until July. It
then suspended *habeas corpus* and arrested the Young Ireland leaders.
Evading the net, O'Brien was persuaded to lead a movement in Tipperary. This soon collapsed after an unsuccessful attempt to dislodge a
party of police ensconced in Widow McCormack's house near
Ballingarry. Briefly on the run, O'Brien was arrested and tried for high
treason in Clonmel with Terence Bellew McManus, Thomas Francis
Meagher and Patrick O'Donohoe. Conviction and sentence to hanging,
drawing and quartering for treason followed inevitably, the prisoners
impressing public opinion by their courageous stance in the dock.

It is doubtful whether O'Brien wanted more than an armed demonstration to bring the British government to reason. Shortly before the
rising he wrote complacently to Lucy about the scenery through which
he was passing [25]. Now the worst fears of his mother were realised.
But the O'Briens refused to abandon their errant relative. The family
turned out in force at Clonmel for the trial. The Dowager Lady
O'Brien, the heavily pregnant Lucy, William's sisters Anne Martineau,
Kate Harris and Grace O'Brien, his brothers Sir Lucius, Robert and
the Rev. Henry, and his bosom friend Woronzow Greig, all lodged in
Clonmel and provided constant moral support. Sir Lucius, though
totally opposed to William's actions, lobbied the government on his
behalf. William's mother, writing to Ellen O'Brien, Robert's wife, on
24 September, before the trial, found consolation in submission to
God's will when considering William's 'perilous' situation. She considered attendance in Clonmel more comforting than remaining at
Dromoland. The dowager was interested to meet Thomas Francis
Meagher, the great Young Ireland orator and later a general in the
American Civil War [28]. Anne Martineau lamented Lucy's tribulations
and reported William's irritation at being tried with McManus and two
unknown farmers [27]. The idea was dropped. The humbler followers
were eventually released, while O'Brien and his leading lieutenants
were tried in succession.

With execution never intended by the government, O'Brien and his colleagues spent a relatively comfortable year imprisoned in Clonmel and in the Kilmainham and Richmond jails in Dublin. They had full access to their families and friends. The commutation of their sentences, by special legislation, to transportation for life to Van Diemen's Land came as a shock, and even the stoical O'Brien wept after bidding farewell to his close relatives in July 1849. At Lucy's suggestion he kept a detailed journal of his life in exile (recently published for the first time),[7] as well as maintaining a copious, if slow, correspondence with family and friends. With the assistance of Robert, who collected the famine-depleted rents, Lucy struggled on, sometimes saving money by taking the children to Dromoland for lengthy visits.

William, unlike his three colleagues and the separately conveyed seditious editors, John Martin, John Mitchel and Kevin Izod O'Doherty, at first refused to accept a ticket-of-leave granting freedom in a restricted area of Van Diemen's Land. Accordingly, for most of 1850 he was kept in close confinement at the penal stations of Maria Island (nine months) and Port Arthur (three months). An escape attempt from the former failed. His mother told him with characteristic bluntness to abandon his childish refusal of a ticket and submit to the authorities [29]. William, moved partly by pressure from friends and partly from the desire to help the Maria Island commandant who had been sacked for kindness to him, finally concurred. Nine months acting as tutor for the motherless sons of an Irish doctor and settler at Red Rock, near Tasmania's Avoca, was followed by his return to a more comfortable and sociable life at a New Norfolk inn. Here O'Brien entertained his friends and made interminable visits to the houses of sympathetic local settlers. He was again irritated when his indefatigable mother, who wrote at enormous length concerning the state of his soul, appealed to the local Anglican archdeacon to preserve him from the theological influence of friendly Catholic priests [30]. William enjoyed more acceptable correspondence with his wife Lucy, his sisters Anne and Grace, and those of his children who were learning to write. Books and mementoes arrived regularly. The still extant necklace of their woven hair entwined in gold, lost between the hotel floorboards, was recovered by an honest Irish maid. To Lucy was accorded the task of editing his journal for publication.[8] In reality his life was not as miserable as his letters home suggested [31]. Some frustration was experienced when O'Brien attempted to guide his family from afar. He insisted that his brilliant son Edward attend Trinity College, Dublin, instead of Cambridge as the latter preferred [30]. Lucy assured her husband that his word was still law when O'Brien feared that he might be disobeyed. Like Sir Edward, Smith O'Brien wanted his son to apply himself to legal studies. O'Brien agreed to his ambitious daughter Lucy studying the classics like her brothers, but insisted that feminine duties must come first [35].

Hoping to placate Irish opinion as Britain drifted towards the Crimean War with Russia, the government announced a conditional pardon for O'Brien, John Martin and Kevin Izod O'Doherty. The other four exiles had escaped from Van Diemen's Land [33]. The released prisoners were now permitted to live anywhere outside British territory. O'Brien had refused to allow his family to come to Van Diemen's Land. Now there were problems of logistics and personnel when Lucy joined him in Brussels [34]. According to unkind family lore, his first words on meeting the family in Brussels were 'What ugly children and what awful brogues.'[9] William was still the remote paterfamilias [35]. In mid-1856 O'Brien took Edward, about to launch his classical career at Trinity College, Dublin, on a tour of Greece. Receiving news of an absolute pardon, William completed the tour for his son's benefit before returning to Ireland to a rapturous welcome from family, friends and the general public [36]. He refused, partly out of consideration for Lucy, to return to parliament, but frequently published his views in the papers. He also travelled throughout the country and abroad, applauded everywhere as a hero.

Shortly after William's restoration to Cahirmoyle his mother fell heavily down a flight of stairs and never recovered, dying at the age of seventy-five. She had played an important role, positively and negatively, in his life. Her death, however, did not provide financial security. In

1848, to avoid the confiscation of his property by the government, William had placed it in trust for Lucy. His brother Sir Lucius, soon to become Lord Inchiquin, and Woronzow Greig were trustees. Lucy naturally allowed him full control over the estate. She was never robust [21], and her death in 1861 left William distraught [37]. Inchiquin and Greig now felt unable to accede to O'Brien's demand for full ownership. A compromise in Chancery gave the estate to his eldest son, Edward, with an annuity of £2,000 for Smith O'Brien. Though now quite wealthy, William was furious with his brother Inchiquin, refusing to meet to him ever again. The long friendship with Greig also seems to have been impaired [38].

Separated from his beloved Cahirmoyle and his local duties, Smith O'Brien assuaged his bitterness in foreign travel and even talked of a return to politics. His daughter Lucy, now Mrs Gwynn, wife of the Warden (i.e. headmaster) of St Columba's College, and his other children endeavoured to find suitable accommodation for their crotchety father [39]. Visiting Wales with his unmarried daughter Charlotte, upon whom he had become increasingly reliant [40], Smith O'Brien died on 18 June 1864.[10] Although the family, many of whom disapproved of William's politics, attempted a quiet funeral, the citizens of Dublin turned out in thousands to bid farewell to their hero.

Smith O'Brien's statue in O'Connell Street, Dublin, mentions only his conviction for high treason. He was also a considerable politician, striving for his country's betterment, and a patron of education, the arts and the Gaelic language. He produced a vigorous family. Edward, an excellent classicist, who rebuilt Cahirmoyle in Italianate splendour, had little or no interest in his father's nationalism. His son Conor, however, ran guns for the Irish Volunteers in 1914, and his daughter Nellie was a keen Gaelic Leaguer and promoter of Irish-speaking schools. Poor Willie died three years after his father as a result of a fall from his horse. Lucy Josephine with her husband, the Very Rev. John Gwynn, subsequently Professor of Divinity at Trinity College, Dublin, was progenitor of a line of scholars and writers. Luckier than his father, Smith

O'Brien lived to see his first grandchild, the distinguished writer and Nationalist MP, Stephen Gwynn. Lucius, the cricketer, became Dean of Limerick, the cathedral founded by his great ancestors. Charles Murrough, born when his father was under sentence of death, died in his twenties. Nationalist identity was maintained in that generation by Charlotte, who proved a tireless campaigner for Irish emigrants and, like her father, a keen student of Gaelic. She worked with Douglas Hyde, subsequently President of Ireland. In the long run, despite the lukewarm patriotism of his siblings and some immediate descendants, William Smith O'Brien succeeded in rescuing his distinguished family from charges of collaborationism and identified it firmly with the coming revolution.

Editorial Note

We have tried as far as possible to retain the original format, spelling and punctuation of the letters. To facilitate reading, however, we have standardised the place and date of each letter on the right of the page. As the dash was the basic punctuation, we have replaced most dashes by more modern forms, retaining them only when clearly expressive; punctuation has occasionally been supplied when the meaning would otherwise have been obscure. Similarly, we have removed some inconsistent or ambiguous capitalisation. Occasional explanatory interpolations are placed within square brackets; missing letters or words are also included within square brackets. We have retained, without comment, original misspellings. Where there is doubt concerning the reading of a particular word or passage, we have inserted a question mark in square brackets. Long paragraphs in the original have been subdivided by paragraph breaks.

As already indicated, the letters are derived from the Smith O'Brien and Inchiquin Papers, housed in the National Library of Ireland, and the private collections of descendants, Dr Robin Gwynn (cited as Robin Gwynn Papers) in New Zealand and Mr Anthony O'Brien (cited as Anthony O'Brien Papers) in Dublin.

Selected Papers of William Smith O'Brien

Woodfield

27 February 1819

My dear William,

When I urged you to chuse the Army in preference to the Navy, it was under the idea that bodily exertion was at least as necessary to you as mental; and that you were fixed on a profession which should ensure danger & give a hope of glory. On reflection, after a more intimate acquaintance; and relying on the correctness of what you write, that you find *a pleasure in study*: I do not hesitate in saying, that considering your talents & expectations; you ought to give up Army & Navy, and finally resolve on qualifying yourself for the Bar. To a young man of good abilities, but above all of persevering industry, with an assured income to enable him to wait at ease its slow rewards, the Law offers every thing that human ambition need aspire to, Rank Fame & Fortune.

The ambitious may look to the Bench the Woolsack, to the names of Mansfield, Erskine, Camden, Thurlow[1] &c &c &c. The avaricious, to the long list of practising barristers, who without patronage, fawning or favour are in the receipt of incomes of from 5 to 15,000 pr ann. The philant[h]ropist & patriot to the opportunity of defending the opprest, and upholding the laws & liberties of his country in the Courts of Justice, & in both houses of parliament. If usefulness be your object, there is no doubt, but that at the Bar & in the House of Commons your opportunities will be more frequent & your sphere of action wider and more various, than either in the Army or Navy. No man doubts the life of Lord Somers to have been useful to his Country, or that the great Lord Chatham, tho' always thwarted & at last driven from the direction of affairs by a jealous & narrow policy, lived in vain. Even lately, in worse times, if Sir Samuel Romilly had lived, what might he not have effected, aided by the experience the public had of the practical utility of his reforms, in those small measures which he extorted from a reluctant & timid Ministry.[2]

Of the value of the achievements of Ma'lbro' & Wellington[3] I will not dispute. A third is not to be found within the Century. Genius & Fortune gave them the power to control events. But every inferior commander relinquishes his free agency and may become, however unwittingly the scourge of his Nation & the enemy of mankind.

Had you less steadiness than I have reason to think, or inferior talents, or were destitu[t]e of fortune & friends, I would advise Army or Navy. Without fortune & of moderate abilities I would say Navy. With talents, volatile, & with only a younger childs portion I would name the Army. As you are, and I write in the Sincerity of real friendship, I do on serious reflection, most earnestly recommend you to decide for the Bar.

Apply yourself to study, to the Classics Greek & Latin, to the Sciences, at least in their Elements. Be not impatient, you will have time enough. Take a broad basis, the building will safely rise the higher; and give a year, at least, to History & political economy at *Edinburgh*. This is a lazy & Luxurious age; the Scotch still retain a good deal of the industry, frugality & hardy habits, of a simpler one.

I[f] after all the harsh aspect of the Law — the study of which is dry, tho' its practice be agreeable enough — should deter you; I would in the next place chuse for *you*, the Army. I think you have talents which may be improved beyond the demands of the Navy. The fate of England, will probably even in your time, be decided by the sword. If you prefer glory to usefulness; be a soldier. You will find abundant opportunity for distinction, and nothing you can acquire need be lost. War is now a science, most complicated. The movement of a great commander shakes the World. To be one you must make yourself an accomplished character. In all the inferior gradations you must rise by being a Courtier & by subserviency.

I am altogether against the Navy. You are too old, & there is no great maritime power for England to cope with, all you would look to, would be some hard knocks in a Frigate with an American.

I shall be very desirous to know your determination; and whatever profession you adopt, my wishes shall follow you, with some anxiety but with much more of hope. Your other friends too expect a good deal from you, you will not grieve & shame us by a disappointment.

You have asked me for my opinion; I feel obliged by the confidence implied, and have given it in sincerity and true friendship

Yours My dear William
faithfully & affecty
J.O'B.

2. *William Smith O'Brien to Charlotte Lady O'Brien*

Harborough Magna
10 March 1819

My Dearest Mamma,

I was very glad to hear that you and all the family are safely arrived at Bath. I daresay you will be rather surprised and I daresay glad to hear that I have entirely given up all thoughts of going into the Navy, I daresay that it seems very fickle in me for 6 months ago I would no more have thought of such a thing than of flying, but I am very glad that I have not been so blinded as to go and I can now clearly see the hand of God in it. It has been rather a trial to me to give up my idol but I have succeeded. The day I received your letter I began to waver, the next day I was decided to go but then after a great deal of consideration I began to perceive gradually that it was best for me to give it up. I am glad that I have not had an opportunity of writing to you on the subject for some time, as time and reflection have strengthened my mind and furnished me with reasons for giving it up. I received a very kind letter from Mr O'Brien which has entirely confirmed me. My reasons for giving it up are —

First I am confident that I shall be able to serve my country much better in some other pursuit and I think that the love of reading and getting knowledge which perhaps I may say, without vanity I have acquired, has been one of the principal reasons for making me think so.

In the next place I am a great deal too old. I should be two and twenty *at least*, before I would be a lieutenant and all that time my mind must have remained inactive as I do not suppose there is such a thing as getting knowledge in a cockpit.

Besides there does not appear to be the least chance of having any thing to do in the Navy, there is no nation now that could put a fleet to sea that would not be beaten in a minute by a few of our ships, so I should have nothing to [do], but be exposed to all the vices and temptations of a cockpit which generally is very little better than a second hell, where I should most likely have not the least religious advantages but perhaps stop out 5 or 6 years without seeing any of my friends. When I consider the pleasure it will give most of my friends to hear that I have given up the Navy, and the benefit that will accrue to myself I cannot be sufficiently thankful, that God has directed me to give it up. I do not mean however to say that the Navy under some circumstances is not a fine profession. I admire the sailors character and I think that the temptations to which one is exposed in it, should not deter any one from going into it when they thought that they should be more useful to their country in it than in any other profession.

As I do not at present know, nor do I particularly wish to know, what I have to depend upon in after life, I shall not fix upon any profession yet as there is plenty of time and the studies that I pursue now will be of use to me in any profession.

I should like to know whether I am to see you at Bath or London before Midsummer, I hope I shall, I should like to spend two or three weeks with you but I could not more, as Mr Scott will not be able to keep me in the holidays. I should like very much to go to Bath as I have not been there for a long time and it is a long time since I have seen Grand Mamma[4] and the Aunts.

Will you my dear Mamma have the goodness to show this list of books to Papa, for his assent to my getting them. [I]t is rather long but then he should remember that I have had scarcely any Classical books since I have been here as I cheifly studied Mathematics &c and [I cannot] do without them, you remember I suppose, that [you pro]mised me I should have Some English books for my re[ading] I should like to have *Robertsons histories* for one and any other books you think proper. —

Cicero	Herodotus
Livy	Demosthenes
Horace	Euripedes
Virgil	Potters Grecian Antiquities
Ainsworths dictionary 4to.	Adam's Roman —do—
	Hederic's Lexicon 4to.

I am very comfortable here at present and should like to stop here very well. [T]here is one thing though I wish I could have done which is that you would ask Mr Scott to let me study in my own room for the other boys make such a noise and sometimes I am sure I should be better able to apply. I am sure he would not have the least objection as I have slightly hinted it to him and he seemed to like it very well. I daresay he is very well satisfied I shall apply as much when I am out of his presence as in. And I want a little money to beautify my room, and to get various little things, I shall stick up the best of my drawings in my room and I still make it as nice a snug little room as any in the three kingdoms. Do ask Mr Scott for this I have many reasons for asking which perhaps I do not like to say. Remember you owe me a pound note and I should have had more had I gone home at Christmas.

I hope I shall see you soon.

Believe me dear Mamma yours very affectionately

William

Give my love to Papa and all the whole tribe of relations that you have at Bath — and pray write to me soon. Forgive my *tediousness* and bad grammar.

3. *William Smith O'Brien to Charlotte Lady O'Brien (at Dromoland)*

> [Harborough Magna]
> Monday [26] September 1819

My dear Mamma,

As I always find that I can write better directly after I receive a letter, than at any other time, I sit Down, to answer your most affectionate letter, which I have just received.

I read the account of Uncle's trial in the papers, and I was very sorry to see that he had lost it, and that deservedly. It is a warning to people not to give way to intemperate anger, and particularly so to me, who am so very apt to get angry about nothing.[5]

With regard to fishing, it is a point which I very often have contested, and though Mr. Scott does not think it wrong, and fishes a good deal himself, yet I am satisfied that it is not justifiable. And here I would remark that I have laid it down, as a principle never to do any thing which I do not think right, merely because other people do it, even if it should be my dearest friend or nearest relation. I do not however say that I should abstain from fishing, because I thought it was wrong; for I do not. The best and indeed the only good argument that I have ever heard brought against it is, that it accustoms a person, to think slightly of giving his fellow creatures pain. When I talk of fishing I mean also shooting for as they are very nearly allied, and the same arguments are brought against both, there is no use in repeating both. I do not understand how fishing can lessen the spirituality of the mind. Hunting, I should think would be *more likely* to do that, as the society which one generally meets with in Hunting is not the best, and far from such as one would wish to associate with. I can easily conceive of *doing nothing* lessening the Spirituality of the mind, as when the mind, is not employed in doing what is good, it will invariably be employed in doing what is not right; but in fishing & shooting you are fully employed, and that in a fine healthy exercise. With regard to myself my love for fishing in itself has entirely subsided, but the question is, how, if you do not fish are you to amuse yourself. You cannot read incessantly and I think that it is the very design of vacation, that the mind should be for a time relaxed, that you may return, with fresh vigour, to the mental pursuits, when the proper time comes. The mind would get stupified were it always in action. Riding is a fine amusement certainly but I can neither ride nor walk without an object in view. Reading something on this very s[ubject] not long ago, I found an advice to young people to ride in at one gate and out at an-other &c. but ask any young man — whether he can feel any pleasure in walking or riding up and down a place, when he has been 500 times before, merely for the sake of exercise and see what he will say. With regard to myself I feel this very much for as I have got nothing to take me yet I am sure that I do not take sufficient exercise for a growing boy. I am, however, thank God very well, and I do not care so long as I do not get stupified. Sometimes I go to bed as tired from reading as if I had walked 20 miles. Enough of fishing &c.

I hope that you have not forgot poor Mr. Devine [?] but have rewarded [him] liberally for his trouble in rising up early and waiting for us &c. I shall be glad if you shall tell me how the poor are getting on about Dromoland, I hope to be able [to] give them something out of my next ten pounds. I began this letter the day I received yours but have not had time to finish it before today Thursday.

Believe me my dearest Mamma Your most
affectionate Son William.

4. *Sir Edward O'Brien to Charlotte Lady O'Brien*

London
2 May 1826

My dear Charlotte,

I am yet unable to fix any day for leaving this. It is supposed that the Disturbances in Lancaster may delay the Dissolution of Parliament.

I have seen Vandeleur several times. He states that he only waits for Sir A. Fitzgerald to come from Paris to accompany him to Ireland.

William intends leaving this for Ireland in a few days, I fear his unfortunate Cambridge Affair will drive all Idea of his going to the Bar out of his Head If he ever was suited to so laborious a profession, which I Much doubt.

I have better hopes of Edward who I intend should go from this to the Netherlands for the summer Months.

I do not feel the least interest in a Parliamentary Life & shall be glad to be released from the trouble of it. Indeed if the Dissolution was not so near I should not return home but get you to meet me in the South of England. As soon as you return home send your carriage immediately to the Coachmaker; to get it Painted and repaired. Let the colour *be Dark*. I think Mr Quinlivan did D. O'Briens carriage up very well — & if we are to go abroad which I fully intend for the winter It will be necessary to put a back seat to it. This can be determined when I go home.

My present intention is to sell all my stock off as fast as they get into order, & not to replace them so as to be able to sell my crops — as the season advances & let my lands — & be entirely disengaged from all Country Pursuits for a year or Two.

From the Description Charlotte Noel gave me of Trent [?] I think it would be a good climate for us to pass this winter in.

> I am your affectionate
> Husband
> Edward O'Brien

5. *Lucius O'Brien to Miss Mary Anne Wilton*

> London
> 28 April 1830

Madam,

I hereby promise in the event of the death of my brother William Smith O'Brien, during our joint lives to continue to you during your life the annuity of Fifty Pounds granted and secured to you by his bond of even date herewith but in the same manner and upon the same terms & conditions as are contained in the Bond and provided that the same annuity be not previously determined, with the proviso that if ever at any time this affair be brought before the Public & Mr William Smith O'Briens name or my own name appear but once in a Public paper as connected with this transaction so long as the annuity be paid my promise shall be void.[6] It is made solely with a view to my Brother's convenience & not from any kind of regard to yourself with whom I am not acquainted or your mother who ought to have taken better care of you. On this day too I shall discharge your brother though I value him as a good & faithful servant & am very sorry to do so & consider every kind of transaction ended between me & any of the members of my family except in the event which this letter contemplates. [*crossed out from 'or your mother' to 'this letter contemplates'*]

> I remain &c
> Lucius O'Brien

6. *Charlotte Lady O'Brien to William Smith O'Brien*

> Dromoland
> 30 March 1835

I can hardly write today

My Dear William,

As I see you are exerting yourself about the relief of our Poor I think it wise to bring before you a few points which have come under my observation in the course of my attention to this subject which you are well aware has been unwearied for the last Twenty five years.

I quite agree with you that Provision for the Sick & Suffering is a bounden Duty but at the same time I am satisfied that such a provision however extended will not better the condition of the people or afford relief to numbers now perishing for want. The great question then is how to arrange a system which will bring all into a State less disgraceful than their present condition & to do this it seems to me necessary to look well to the primary causes of the distress we witness.

I could go back for many years to find examples in the subjects I would speak on but shall take these now before me & can hardly give you a stronger proof of the insufficiency of your plan than the case of a Family now in Newmarket where I have at much expence opened a trade for the female poor which Languishes for want of hands & not from want of power to give employment. The case is that of a weaver & his wife with four children. The man is able to work the woman is able to Draw Turf & potatoes on her back being remarkably Large & Strong. The children are all grown up except one girl of nine who if she had attended the work school might now receive 1/6 or 2s a week, & yet they are without furniture, bedding, Clothes and I believe food as they are Continually Sending here for Alms. Now what is to be done with such a family as this, & who could have insisted on their children learning to work before they were too old & too much established in Idle habits to attempt — Under your Bill a Family of this kind could get no relief & yet they must go out as beggars unless something is done for them & they are old inhabitants of the Town & Roman Catholics who consequently are not injured by exclusive dealing or persecution like the poor protestants.

Well in other instances families have commenced well in life made money & had all flourishing about them. When feeling at ease they began *treating* themselves or their Neighbours &, soon get into difficulties by expending in Punch what might have made every thing about them neat & Comfortable. After struggling some years in the greatest apparent Misery having sent Article after Article to the pawn office they Apply to the next resident gentleman, get relief on a more kind & extensive scale than you are inclined to admit in your Testimony to great Britain respecting us, Send those things received in this way after the others to the Pawn office & having drained all around them until it was evident half their estates could do them no good Set out with half a dozn. children like moving Bundles of rags to prey upon those poor who may have been more provident than themselves.

This that I have set before you is neither an extreme nor a Singular case. It is the history of more than half the Families who give such an appearance of wretchedness to this Country — & how the evil is to be checked until you can Convince the people that their idle dissipated habits are the real cause of the misery of the Country I am quite at a loss to say for in every district there are not merely hundreds but even thousands who would only increase their Self indulgence if in falling into distress they had a prospect of Parish relief, & very very few comparatively who if they are by industry enabled to make a little money will lay it over in any way tending to give a civilized Comfortable appearance to the Country.

I will not multiply cases branching out from these, which will naturally occur to your own mind, but try to explain to you that as far as I can Judge the establishing mendicities for shutting up vagrants who are now most injurious to the peace as well as to the Comfort of the industrious part of the Community & the putting down Ale houses would in my mind tend more to the benefit of Ireland than any thing that can be done. The aged & infirm poor tho suffering themselves from want of Comforts one would wish to see extended to them are not the Cause of the Misery we see in the Country & I may say that the poverty of one Family in ten does not arise from the burden of maintaining their helpless relatives but either from want of employment, from *unwillingness to avail themselves* of *the Species of employment set before them*, or from Love of dissapation & amusement Low & idle as it is & scarcely appearing amusement in our eyes.

If you can devise some remedy for these things & can really separate between the Humble deserving poor & the Sturdy brawling *evil minded Mendicant* who is much oftener relieved *thro fear* than thro Charity you will do infinite good to your Country. And having been always an advocate for poor Laws & certain the present state of mendicancy in the Country Rather tends to harden than to soften the hearts of those *well acquainted* with it, I would not advocate the leaving a Single Individual to casual charity tho I would the taxing both real & *personal* property so as to secure permanent relief for the afflicted.

I shall not touch on other Topics wishing you to Consider this deeply & to reflect how little you will effect unless you enforce industry & suppress vagrancy & that possible waste of Money which enriches none but t[hose] who generally end their days as mendicants or in the Colonies *under the protection of Government*.

I hope Dear Lucy is well. I wish she was in some cheerful Street near Westminster where she would be more in the way than at Wilton St. I always felt the difference when I moved away from the House to have the appearance of a better Habitation & was much happier Lodging at a tailors in half Moon St. than when residing in Lord Beglys house in Welbeck St. Pray think of this for dear Lucy & dont let her be too Lonely, tho she may appear cheerful when you come home the mind will sink under it.

Yr. affect. Mother
C.O'B.

I feel quite unable to give you my ideas in a Fine condensced or regular form & can only hope you will be able to understand them & excuse the very bad state in which they appear before you.

7. *Anne O'Brien [later Martineau] to Lucy O'Brien*

[Dromoland]
[9 March 1837]

My dearest Lucy,

You must have a line tho' I can only tell you that we are all very unhappy about poor dear Papa & have written for the 3 brothers. He is in such a happy composed state of Mind that we can only thank God for calming every trouble away before this time arrived. I trust your poor baby is better. May God bless you & may we all be enabled to say his will be done.

Your most attached
Anne
(to 78 George St, Limerick)

Dear Mrs Gabbett,

Give this to Lucy if you like

Your aff—
A

8. *Anne O'Brien to Lucy O'Brien*

> Dromoland
> Friday 10 oclock [March 1837]

Dearest Lucy,

I am thankful to say the dear father lives but alas gets weaker & weaker. He is composed & happy but wishes much his absent sons were with him & said today he should like very much to see Williams child. Now dearest Lucy do not let this wish influence you for one moment to come if you think it may be attended with any injury to you or the dear baby but if Dr Griffin[7] & Mrs Gabbett think that with perfect safety you might come out in the Landau we will send it in tomorrow after post time if it still pleases God to spare the dear Father so long. Mamma wanted me to say Monday but she has too much hope — & thinks there is more time than any one else does — you should consider well whether you are strong enough to come into the midst of a scene of sorrow — and all that is yet to come which I dread to think of. In short you must let others decide for you. We should be delighted to have you and we think Dromoland always agrees with you but Dromoland is not itself now — then Dr Frazer's experience about children & success with them makes us wish dear Baby was in his hands but you must not say this — I keep on hoping they may have left London. [W]e have had no letter for some days from either W— [William] or E— [Edward]. Write & tell us what W— says — he must have had time to answer my first sad account of Papa written on Saturday.

My head aches so you must excuse this. Kate & Ellen are not worse Much the same no great amendment Can be expected under present circumstances.

God be with you & keep your poor dear child from harm. Ever your most affect sister.

> Anne O'Brien

9. *Charlotte Lady O'Brien to Lucy O'Brien* (*at 78 George's Street, Limerick*)

Dromoland
Tuesday [7 March 1837]

My Dearest Lucy,

I am much grieved to hear that your child has been ill & altho' under gt anxiety of mind about Sir Edward who is very ill in Influenza I write at once to say that you can never expect to have your child thriving & healthy as the people about here say while at so early an age you give it the milk of two persons. Such an arrangement might not injure it perhaps at 6 or 7 months but is very bad for it when young & I do think you should either give up the pleasure of nursing which under yr circumstances would be best & leave it entirely to the Nurse or Suckle it yourself only feeding it very lightly with Panada. I never gave my children that were suckled any thing whatever but the Nurses milk until they were very near being weaned — & was very careful not to let the Nurse eat green vegetables or salt meat — they were all very healthy & fat. If you have a good Nurse let me entreat you to pursue this plan & you will see the benefit of it in a few days please GOD — It is very possible your own Milk may not agree with the child & as it is delicate you had better leave it to the Nurse than try to rear it y^r· self. Whatever you do pray dont let it get too much or a variety of food — instead of fattening the Baby it will only give it Inward pains & convulsions. I had my Directions from one of the Best Physicians for Ladies & Chil[dren] I ever met.

I think you had better not come to us while the Influenza is so rife & of so severe a character in this House.

Docr Frazer is just come in & quite agrees with me about yr child & Instances one in this neighbourhood. Only he is most decided that you should leave it to the Nurse because y^r own anxiety will injure it.

Pray shew this to Mrs Gabbett & believe me y^r very affect.

C. O'Brien

10. *William Smith O'Brien to Lucy O'Brien*

London
24 July 1838

My Darling Lucy,

The interesting intelligence which has been hinted in former letters and directly conveyed in that received this morning calls forth many reflections of a serious nature, as well as a sentiment of gratitude for what is generally though not always very justly regarded as a Boon.

In the light of a Boon however I shall consider an accession to the numbers of our little family, and I trust that we shall neither of us ever have occasion to consider it otherwise. Should the event which you anticipate take place it must bring to a crisis the question of Parliament versus Income. If I were in doubt (and I have lately entertained very serious doubts) whether even without such an income I ought not to abstain from encountering the expenses of another session without an increase of income, that doubt will be converted into a certainty as you are fully assured that we may expect a new visitor into this world of troubles, next Spring. In fact I may say now that in such an event I have made up my mind to give up my seat unless my mother shall give me a gross income of £1000 per ann — otherwise I should be under the necessity of leaving you in Ireland during nearly the whole of next Session.

We shall have abundance of time however to consider what is best to be done before January next.

I was in the House all day yesterday morning at Com[mencement] and evening about the Tithe arrears I felt myself compelled by a sense of justice to give a vote against the Governmt which will not increase my popularity with my constituents. However I am sure that upon all occasions it is better to *act justly* whether approbation or disapproval be the result.[8]

Yrs most affly
husbd
William S. O'Brien

11. *Charlotte, Dowager Lady O'Brien, to William Smith O'Brien*

Elendon
13 August 1838

My Dear William,

I have been so much in company since the receipt of your last letter from London that I could not write with any comfort & now take only a hurried hour previous to my journey by the rail road to Whitkirk — we have had a very comfortable fortnight since we left Farnborough — The Martineaus were kind as possible & a very pleasing Family; being in the same house with dear Kate & her Baby was a great comfort to me & I saw more of its little ways the three days it was at Basing park than the whole month at Farnborough. It is a very nice child & good tempered scarcely even crying & strong to [*tho'*] small. It cut two teeth at Basing park which was great delight to papa & Mamma. I hope you found dear Lucy & your Boy well & that you are by this time comfortably settled at Carmoyle [*Cahirmoyle*] & found everything in good order. It had been my intention as soon as I found myself in a situation to spend any money there & put a question to you but since you have written to me on the subject I shall not wait for that period but at once enquire what your views & intentions are with respect to making it your residence. You are well aware it has always been my opinion that if you were in possession of the whole estate you could not afford to keep up the place as a residence suited to the property & spend part of each year in London. I saw enough of such a system in early life to feel certain that one or other must be given up or that you would be involved in debts you would never possess the means of paying. It is therefore of great importance before anyone lays out money at Carmoyle that your views should be brought to a distinct conclusion otherwise it will be only throwing it away.

As to what you say with regard to the duty of keeping up Carmoyle as a Family residence I cannot at all agree with you. It never was any thing more than a Farm purchased by my Father who was a second son & made by his own labour every shilling he possessed. The House never was near as good during his life *as it was when given up to you* & he considered it so little fit for a residence that he never took any of us there after I was eleven years of age & in fact let the whole place go to ruin giving it to Bridget Keevan[9] for a Dairy & letting the cows into every part of it that my mother had tried to make neat as you have done.

When I passed Carmoyle in 1830 the full conviction on my mind was that it should be left to Mr. Massy as a farm, and a residence, if one was required, made on a more favourable & *less remote* part of the Estate & your marriage changed my views on this subject & I considered to have the place taken up for you as you seemed to think of it the part of the estate you could best like to reside on; & had so decidedly declared your intention of abandoning parliament & devoting yourself to the improvement of the country & your own future property.

The circumstances of your being so long without a child most probably changed your feelings & made you careless about becoming a good country gentleman & as long as you had no prospect of a family no one could be surprized at it. I own however that your *last* acceptance of the proposal of standing for the County — together with yr. readiness to let Carmoyle even to a stranger that you might spend much of yr. time in London have so revived my doubts as to its being a place either you or your son who will be educated in England, will really make a residence that I often regret its having been taken up for you; & altho when I am there, I should like to have something going on for my amusement, must ever feel that it is but throwing away what might be better applied.

Under these circumstances I would rather not continue the Back fence at present or lay out more there than is absolutely necessary to keep all as you gave it to Me. When I am there in spring I will consider how to act respecting it & possibly by that time your plans of future life will be more fixed than at present.

When you have time to look about you at Carmoyle I shall be much obliged by your telling me soon what repairs are absolutely necessary & hope you will get everything estimated for me on the most economic scale as I can undertake nothing in the way of expence until I have made your Brothers who are so poor and working so hard for what they do possess, a little more comfortable.

I enclose a letter with money which I shall be obliged to you to forward carefully; you franked a letter for Robt to yr aunt here & mine to her has never reached. This is for a Daughter of yr uncle George Stevelly's & I am anxious she should get it soon.

Believe me my Dear William with kind love to Lucy & Baby & best wishes for both your very affect Mother,

C. O'Brien

12. *William Smith O'Brien to Lucy O'Brien*

London
20 August 1841

My Dearest Lucy,

I was beginning to get into very low spirits when your letter written on Wednesday reached me & has revived my spirits. Truly I was not favoured by the *idiosyncrasy* of my nature to be alone. The solitude of London is worse than that of a wilderness. It is true I meet plenty of acquaintances When I go out — all of whom are very kind — but the companion of the domestic Home is wanted. This feeling is aggravated by the absence of all occupation. Indeed now that I reflect upon my Conduct I am at a loss to know what brought me here so much sooner than was needed, for I might have known that there would be no division on the Speakership — so that I might have remained at home several days longer without injury to any one & with much benefit to myself & satisfaction to others. As for Amusement I have for three successive evenings determined to go to the Haymarket & then has my zeal failed when I bethought me of the bore of sitting for three or four mortal Hours stewing in a play House listening to a drama which would perhaps raise no feelings of pleasure. London is excessively empty. Not a carriage to be seen, a few straggling MPs looking [?] excessively dismal at being brought up from their homes. It seems however to be the impression of every one that this little interlude of session will not last long.

Mrs. Greig is staying out of town at Twickenham. She left a note for me supposing that I should go to Belgrave St.

I saw William Lillingstone today for the first time since 1832. He is a strange creature, but an amiable man.

I have also met Augustus O'Brien[10] who is not a little pleased with his accession of dignity. I shall be rather curious to watch what course he will take in the House.

The debate on the address is expected to continue for some days. These long debates are excessively tiresome.

I am much interested by what you tell me about Edwards little prayer. May it avail! God knows I ought not to be insensible to the value of the prayers of others for I find it very difficult to pray for myself.

I hope that you will not let Mr or Mrs Gabbett[11] depart for another fortnight. I hope to be with you before the 10th of September as I shall probably attend the Banquet to be given to Lord Morpeth[12] on the 9th in Dublin.

> Give affect. Love to all & believe
> me yrs. evr affectly
> W.O'B.

13. *William Smith O'Brien to Lucy O'Brien*

> London
> 21 March 1843

My Dearest Lucy,

Though you scarcely deserve a line from me — having neglected to write your usual Journal, I do not like to allow another day to pass without scribbling a few words. You ought to take this determination as a great compliment because my motion stands on the Paper for tonight. Still it is uncertain whether I shall be able to bring it on, it not being put in the list. How vexatious are these delays & uncertainties. Such however is the fate of all who meddle in affairs of high import.[13]

They cannot command time & circumstances & I am consoled sometimes by seeing older & abler men than myself equally frustrated.

Without such agitations Life would become a stagnant Pool. As for my own personal labour I care very little about it so long as I perceive any movement in those affairs about which I am interested. I sometimes fancy indeed that I could be satisfied — ambitious though I am — fond of applause also — that my name should never be mentioned if I could feel that I was really advancing useful ends by my labours. But to toil on perpetually without making any progress, to surrender all the enjoyments of ease & of a peaceful life without effecting any useful results is a torment such as has been represented in ancient fable by the story of Sisyphus & his stone. If I get over my motion tonight I shall be able to leave town sooner than if it be postponed, but I do not wish to fix any day lest you may be disappointed.

I went to the Speakers Levee on Saturday last. Nothing else new. I have been quite absorbed in my French novel Consuelo[14] of which I have obtained two more volumes, without however coming to an end. It interests me wonderfully I scarcely know why.

> God bless you dearest
> Kiss the children for me &
> fare you well — Yrs W.O'B.

14. *Charlotte, Dowager Lady O'Brien, to William Smith O'Brien*

> Dromoland
> 24 October 1843

My Dear William,

Your kind note gave me great pleasure when I received it yesterday & I was beginning to calculate how soon I might have the pleasure of seeing you & Lucy & your dear Children at that place in which I so much like to dwell for a little time every year when the enclosed paragraph from the Times in conjunction with your letter to Lucius dispelled the delusion. And now what can I say to my dear Child but to warn him once more as to the course he is pursuing.

I have long seen & felt the great evil of the repeal agitation to *my poor Country men* & even a child must know that nothing but misery & wretchedness and increased want of employment could follow a separation between Great Britain & Ireland even supposing it to be effected without Bloodshed Anarchy & Confusion. But the Queens Speech & the late proceedings have put beyond all doubt the light in which the attempt to bring it about is to be regarded. And it is most Selfish & reckless & Heartless towards your wife & children, to say nothing of yr. Mother & Brothers and Sisters, to proclaim yourself a Rebel & a supporter of Rebels when up to the present time you were known not to be a repealer. This Act of yours my dear William if it be accomplished (which God forbid it is) places all your Friends, & especially your affectionately attached Mother in a most painful situation; & there is no saying what the consequence of it may be to yourself & to yr. Family. I will not however anticipate evil but simply give this warning — That I never will either directly or indirectly pay a shilling towards the defence of a State prosecution — And must defer signing the Settlement I was going to make for your Children until a sufficient length of time has passed to give me full assurance that there is no danger your property may be confiscated.

Farewell — If you pursue the course announced in the papers you will bring down my Grey head with Sorrow to the Grave but however sorrowing I shall never cease to be your

fondly attached Mother
C. O'Brien

15. *Charlotte, Dowager Lady O'Brien, to William Smith O'Brien*

Dromoland
Christmas Day [1843]

Remonstrance

On this day when we commemorate that great event which alone gives hope of meeting in happiness hereafter I will make one effort more to separate my beloved child from the unholy association he has this year

formed with men who have no object in view but their own advance-
ment & the destruction of that form of Religion which renounces their
errors, and teaches us to worship God in Spirit & in Truth, with the
heart & understanding, not in forms & ceremonies & vain delusions

[rest of leaf torn off]

of political conduct you have adopted; But I will make the effort —
And as I would if I met you, clasp your Knees & hold you fast until I
extracted a promise that you would separate yourself from these
ungodly men, I now upon the bended knees of an aching heart entreat
you to *have nothing more to do with them.*

The thought of your going to Dublin to join in consultation &
Friendship with the mischievous character who penned the last letter
against the Landlord & Tenant Commission; and with such degraded,
ill-conducted characters as Mr. John P. [?] Molony[15]

[rest of leaf torn off]

if you could but hear the way in which you are spoken of & mourned
over by those who once expected their party to derive great good from
your fathers industry & moderation; you would indeed hesitate before
you defied Public Opinion, & ran into a line of conduct which can only
end in ruin to yourself & your children.

Once more then Dearest William I would entreat you by every tie, by
every feeling, by every argument a Mother can use, to give up this *unsuit-
able* — this unholy — this wicked alliance — And to wait in quiet &
retirement, either at Cahirmoyle, or with your Family on the Continent

[rest of leaf torn off]

say, your wisdom at present is, to be still.

This is probably the last time I shall prefer any request on this subject, but my heart will follow you with anxious thought wherever you
go — and Oh may it be to find comfort & not misery, for you cannot
make me unhappy without making yourself your wife and your children unhappy also.

Farewell — May God's peace & Blessing rest upon your house at this Holy Season & may He, with the strength of His Holy Arm — deliver you from the grasp of that enemy who desires to take you Captive at his will that he may destroy both body & Soul.

> Under all circumstances believe me
> your tenderly affectionate

[rest of leaf torn off]

16. *Lucy O'Brien to William Smith O'Brien*

> Cahirmoyle
> 13th [January 1844]

Lucius 1 year & 6 months old today

My dearest William,

I am dying to know what you are doing in Dublin. I am in such a fright about you since I heard that O'Connell is convicted for which strange to say I am really sorry putting you out of the question. Papa came here yesterday for my mother. Instead of her going home they remain here for some days. He has brought us all the Conservative talk whilst mother is in heart a thorough repealer & I am a trembler for my husband. The servants in this house are in such a state about it & I am told all Rathkeale is in a ferment. We have not yet seen the paper but hope to do so tonight.

The children are going on well no measles, Ned still delicate, Willy with a cough, but I am told it is not of the least of consequence as it is a constant attendant on the measles.

I think I have grown rather fat since you left me.

The men are busy at the drain near Maguires [?] fields, Owen almost disabled poor man. We never see any company so that I have not anything to tell. Every day I have various Messages from your little girl to you which I leave you to Imagine. She wants to travel up by the coach to you to keep your house & sends you four loves & three kisses & two kisses & one love to uncle Robert.[16] Is he a Repealer? Your attached & most anxious wife & friend.

Lucy C. O'Brien

17. *Lucy O'Brien to William Smith O'Brien*

Cahirmoyle fireside
Monday evening [22 January 1844]

Have you bought yourself a Knife?

My dearest William,

Your letter today gave me great pleasure but I wish you were settled in nice clean & elegant lodgings pray do not spare upon yourself but make yourself comfortable. I hope you will go to many literary meetings &c. It will beguile the long & lonely evenings. I don't feel half so much for you in London as I know you are there Employed after five. Your letter arrived today whilst we were all at dinner & at 3p.m. I am teaching the children manners at long dinners & Mamma chooses to be one with me. Great was the rejoicing at a letter from dear papa & many the questions. We are very lonely indeed without you. Perhaps you will think me odd when I say that I would rather be *quite* alone with my children at present but it is very kind of dr Mamma to come with me she returns home on Monday at latest. Papa comes for her on Saturday. I feel so uneasy that I like to be by myself. Please to send me a paper regularly it is too anxious a time to do without one. I saw your mother she spoke with much affection of you & was I think disappointed at not having been visited by you but perhaps it was for the best; she looks very well indeed. All thought of her going at present to Kate[17] is over. She has sent her money instead to assist her in taking a house. I think the accounts of Henry are more satisfactory on the whole. I have had a letter from Mrs Greig[18] & will send it you it is a sad one indeed & I hope wont put you *out* but please return it to me & dont tell her you read it. I send you also a paper about the policy of Insurance I hope you will allow the £144.14/4 to be added to the sum promised for our children's benefit.[19] Joe[20] gave it me for you. I found all flourishing on my return home. Captain has not yet gone to Enrights as his back is sore. It would be a pity to risk spoiling him for a few stone more of oats. The coals have been all delivered except 2 ton. No other news from home. Owen is hard at work cropping the trees &c in the flower garden. Edward read his Homer to me today. Tomorrow Mr Dillon comes to us. Can you yet tell me what you are likely to do about going to town or my going to you or a house or what if you are lonely shall we not go to you? You will receive this note written Monday night on Wednesday morning Edward's birthday. Dont forget the dear child & us all we *will* all send extra thoughts to you.

No increase in the family at home!

Thank you for any kindness to my dear Robert his conversation will repay you if you try for it & it will remind you of our Ned. Give Robert Mammas & my best love. She will write soon to him. Was there any good speaking at the Trial[21] & what are you doing. Please pay Louisa for me. I must write to her but you are to pay [*illegible*].

God bless you dearest. I do not forget to pray for you Night & Morning nor have we forgotten the family petition I hope you will continue it alone.

Your most affectly attached wife Lucy.

Michael is to send your boxes by canal to 82 Lower Mt St on Wednesday next D.G.

Lucy looks well & fresh once more. Mamma is much pleased with her. She [Lucy Josephine] says 'I must not speak with a brogue because papa w^d not like his little girl to be Miss Blake.'

18. *William Smith O'Brien to Lucy O'Brien (at Cahirmoyle)*

[Dublin]
4 March 1844

My Dearest Lucy,

I am very angry with you for repining at the prospect of an accession to the family [Robert Donough]. Poor Mrs John Waller lost one of her children the other day. Perhaps if it were the will of Providence to desire of us of a portion of present treasure we should be truly thankful to have our later days consoled by the survivor. Welcome therefore the burden instead of regretting it.

Finding that the gentleman who occupies the drawing room floor of this House has left town for two months I am decidedly in favor of your coming up here without delay as I can obtain his rooms for £1: per week additional for you alone & 1:12.6 with rest of family.

If you come alone I shall expect you to stay till Easter if not longer. I leave to your own discretion to choose any of the three following plans.

1. To come alone —
    extra expense of visit to Dublin dress inclusive say £30 to £40
2. To bring Mary & Edward along with you *in day coach* —
    say £40 to 50.
3. To bring carriage with Richard Mary Edwd Willy & Lucy[22]
    say £60 to £80 — the whole party remaining for two months —
I am myself strongly in favor of the latter of these schemes —

If you come up in the Carriage take care that the wheels are oiled before you leave Limerick. Let me hear from you by return of Post on the subject. You will require to take two days for your journey if you Come in the carriage.

My landlady says that it will not be necessary that you should bring Plate or Linen.

I will send you an order in Limerick for as much money as you may want. As I cannot hear from you before Thursday I will send an order on Hunter to Limerick for £30. £10 ought to pay your expenses to

Dublin but you will do well to reserve £15 or £20 for the journey in case of accidents.——

Yrs ever affectly
W.S.O'B.

If you leave Cahirmoyle on Wednesday or Thursday you can be here on Friday or Saturd[ay.] I recommend you to leave on Wednesday afternoon — & to start from Limk on Thursday so [as to] reach Roscrea or Maryborough on Thursday.

Take care to write to me, both from Cahirmoyle & from Limerick so that I may know when to expect you & to make arrangements about the Carriage &c.

19. *William Smith O'Brien to Charlotte, Dowager Lady O'Brien*

Lisnaskea
Blackrock
18 March 1845

My Dear Mother,

You could not give a better illustration of a disposition to misinterpret everything which falls from me than in misapplying expressions which you may have discovered in some speech or publication of mine.

Conscious that the efforts made by me to serve the unhappy land which is neglected so much by those who owe it the various duties incidental to the possession of Property have rendered it impossible for us to meet or to correspond without mutual pain to each other I should not have broken the silence which has been thus forced upon me if it were not that this affair of Mrs Brews[23] appears to me to wear a very serious aspect — first in reference to character, and next chance of a most disagreeable lawsuit.

In regard to the first point I need not repeat that every member of the family would deeply grieve if a lawsuit should bring to light any neglect of her interests.

20. *Charlotte, Dowager Lady O'Brien, to William Smith O'Brien*

[Dromoland]
18 March 1845

Just sent to Wm Sunday March 31

My Dear W,

I do not know on what premise of interpretation of thoughts or words you conclude yrs. of 20th [18th?] by saying that you know whatever proceeds from yr. lips or from yr. pen is likely to be misconstrued or misinterpreted by me. I am not aware of having at any time put any other meaning on words that grieved or distressed me but what you have publicly avowed to the whole world & & my chief desire is to shut my eyes & ears to what you say & do until you are separate from those who have taught you to profess publicly that it is our country mens duty to treat with 'bitter scorn' all who think as I think respecting the ignus fatuus which is separating you from those who really love you, & would prove much truer friends in sorrow or affliction than your new associates.

But I do not write with the intention of opening any correspondence on these subjects but simply to make known to you feelings very similar to yr own on a most distressing subject which W.F. [William Furlong, lawyer] well knows has harrassed me ever since I found that Mrs Brew was in distress & that there was such a difficulty as law causes to exist in my giving her relief.

21. *Lucy O'Brien to William Smith O'Brien*

[Cahirmoyle]
St Patrick's Day [1846]

My dear William,

I am rather better but very very absurdly weak & as yet unable to do more than to give my love & the little ones to their dear papa. Robert came on Sunday and returned to Limerick last night. He will not be returning at Stachallan as he does not get on with the Warden &

disapproves of compulsory fasts, etc.[24] Edward is well as can be. I must get him to write. Too tired for much more.

Your aff. Lucy

22. *William Smith O' Brien to Lucy O'Brien*

House of Commons Prison
6 May 1846

My Dearest Wife,

I send you a satisfactory note from Nancy, about Willy.[25]

I find Prison agrees with me very well.

I am in a 'towering passion' this morning on reading the proceedings of the Association.

The O'Connell *creatures* there have paralysed the expression of opinion so that the Association has withheld approval of my Conduct.

I have written to Dr Costello[26] to intimate that I shall resign my seat as soon as my imprisonment is terminated by the act of the House.

What have you done about the painting of the House. You may as well make arrangements with Mr McNulty without delay.

Get an estimate from him before you make any agreement.

Henry [brother] is here, so also Kate & Charles. I am overpowered with visitors.

Believe me
Ever most affectly
W.O'B.

23. *Lucy O'Brien to William Smith O'Brien*

Cahermoyle
8 May 1846

My dearest William,

I am boiling over with indignation at the way in which 'that clique' has treated you. I cannot persuade myself that they represent the nation but only the cunning & jealous mind of the Master. If however there is not a general expression of disavowal of the Association I am sure you are quite right to have done with them for the *present*. You can well afford to bide your time for a truer spirit. Pray send me the *Nations* Oh! for Mr. Davis.[27] My mother is indignant beyond measure but confounds all Irishmen in her denunciations whilst I confine it to a few. As to the Maids words cannot express their rage. The trades people at Newcastle & Rathkeale are most vehement in your support. Are you really likely to be confined for months & is it true that it will cost you £2,000 a childs fortune? but think not I cry *cave*.

Thanks for sending me Nancy's letter. Richard I expect tonight & will tell you what he says of dear Willy. I am most anxious to hear all about him. I sent you Mr Nulty's estimate & will get Upton to work next week also the plasterer as he is wanted to plaster some spots before the new paper is put up. May I get him to plaster the W.C. & the place the old Linney way in. If you surrender will you spend the winter with me in Italy? & *Lilly*

Your most affte Lucy —

24. *Charlotte, Dowager Lady O'Brien, to William Smith O'Brien*

[Dromoland]
25 February 1847

My Dearest William,

If it be true that the Government are going (as Stated in the last London papers) to send over Mr Soyer[28] of the reform Club to establish soup Kitchens in Ireland. The Irish Members who are acquainted with the Country & the habits of the people ought to wait on them without delay to represent the waste of money which must attend an undertaking of the kind & the total impracticability of carrying it into execution. From the experience we have all round us in this country of Soup Kitchens you may rest assured that the people could never be satisfied with the kind of Soup Mr Soyer speaks of making. And that those most in want of food would not or could not take their families to eat it at the Kitchens spoken of. They have no clothes to leave their Houses altogether & would rather have a cake of coarse bread or a quart of thick Porridge to take home to their Children than a Gallon of Soup. Indeed it is now clearly proved that Soup in itself is not sufficient to satisfy the Stomach used to potatoes. It requires some[thing] Solid to fill it & even to the poor women who sit at home at Newmarket they are obliged to give a piece of Meat with the soup to induce them to come for it altho it is thickened with meal & given gratis. I write off to you in the greatest haste about this business that if it be real — & not a hoax as some say, — an effort may be made to show how the money spent in London on Cooking aparatus & travelling kitchens will be completely thrown away while the same sums given in Bean Meal cakes *such as we used to make here* or Indian Meal &c &c would feed thousands.

I am my Dear William
Yr very affect. Mother
C. O'Brien

25. *William Smith O'Brien to Lucy O'Brien*

Bantry
9 July 1848

My Dearest Wife,

At length I have obtained a moment of repose which enables me to write you a line — Without delaying you by telling how grieved I was leaving my cherished home and my little circle of six — M, W, E, L, C, D, L, — R, N [*arranged in a circle*][29] with Mamma presiding I shall proceed to narrate my adventures. Arrived in Newcastle nearly an hour too soon — obtained an outside place — day windy but not disagreeable — met near Killarney by Mr Shine Lawlor[30] — party in the evening of Repealers. Next day went to Rossbeigh, a watering place on Dingle Bay where Mr Lawlor's family are now abiding for benefit of sea air. Mrs Lawlor (an Englishwoman) returned with us. Let me here

observe that I wish you could ask her and her husband to Cahirmoyle.
He is a man of high Education, of good property, of gentlemanly
demeanour, not merely an agitator like your poor husband, but also an
excellent country Gentleman such as you desire me to be: attends sessions, Boards of Guardians, Grand Juries, drains land Farms &c and has
a very nice house on the Lake of Killarney in one of the prettiest spots
in Europe. An occasional exchange of visits wd be very agreeable to
you. I am afraid however Mr Shine Lawlor is nearly as far on his way to
Bermuda[31] as myself. He does not think it a sin even for a man with
four children & good inheritance to be guilty of the 'felonious' act of
loving his country, and of being prepared if necessary to die for it.
When at Rossbeigh I could not help wishing that you were settled there
for a few weeks. The strand is most inviting for bathing, the scenery
grand, but unfortunately it is a solitary Spot. You could obtain two
lodges for £8 per month. i.e. £4 each but it is necessary to provide beds
& other articles of furniture. For beef &c you would be compelled to
send to Killarney or Cahircivin. From Castle Lurgh I proceeded accompanied by Mr Shine Lawlor & Mr Shea Lawlor[32] to Bearehaven, the
remotest burgh of the County of Kerry [*recte Cork*]. We passed through
Kenmare. Stopped to breakfast at the House of Father John, the Priest,
and were received with a demonstration by the People of Kenmare. We
addressed them in terms appropriate to the occasion. The road from
Kenmare to Castle Town (Bearehaven) passes through a very wild
romantic Country. We stopped at the House of a Mr McFinnans
[Feane?] a gentleman of small property who lives about half way and
from there went to see a 'pattern' which interested us beyond measure
— At a pla[ce] & called Lurgh na Quinlin [?] there is a small lake upon
which there are tussocks which occasionally move about the Lake. The
peasants of the neighbourhood believe that the lake is sacred and all
these tussocks are moved by spiritual agency. They therefore upon the
commencing of the 'pattern'[33] visit it in successive numbers, dip in it
persons & children afflicted with sickness. They go their 'rounds' at an
altar placed upon a little hill near the lake. Nothing could be more picturesque than the scene. I stand in a ruined churchyard. In the fore-

ground the lake with groups of peasantry in the act of dipping their children and sprinkling themselves with the water of the blessed lake. Close by a small Hill surrounded by a ring of people moving rapidly in circuit with uplifted hands. Additional Parties arriving at each moment. Occasionally a whole family is to be seen on the back of a Kerry pony. The cavalcade of equestrians remind one of the picture in which the Arabs are seen passing through the rocky Interiors of the Desert. The whole scene encircled on the one side by the Sea on the other by bold & majestic mountains. It was a scene which Grace and you would have enjoyed as Errors of the picturesque, but in regard to the personal & religious effects of the meeting I say nothing. Whether it be for their advantage that many thousands should spend long nights either under the canopy of heaven or under the Canopy of tents surrounded by all the usual temptations which are accessories to a scene such as this is a Question which I leave the formalist to decide. As for what is called 'the superstition' of the case You know that I am of opinion that it is better to believe a great deal too much than to [believe *crossed out*] than to fall short over a little in credulity. I therefore am disposed to hope that the all seeing eye will receive with as much acceptance the humble believers of faith carried by the Kerry peasant as was in former times accorded to the Visitants at the Pools of Bethseda & of Silvan. Proceeding through this romantic country we arrived about eleven o'clock at Castletown where to my astonishmt I found an hotel as large as the House of Mr Kennedy at Rathkeale & better furnished — Castletown is situated immediately opposite to Bear island and is the Spot which Enters into Competition with Valencia as a Port desired for trans Atlantic communication. I am compelled to give it the preference & hope to see the time when if not through our own Glorious Shannon, through this emporium will pass the communication of Europe with the entire Hemisphere. Yesterday morning I rode about eight miles & back to visit the Copper mines at Alliheis near Dursey island — Upon our return we addressed an assemblage of People at Castle Town — I have not time to tell you all about O'Sullivan Bear and his Castle at Dunboy but if you feel any interest respecting these things turn to the

Poems of Davis & your imagination will supply the rest. From Castle town we went to Glengariff (Oh how I wish that you were comfortably settled at an Hotel there for a few weeks) where we were received by the Bantry Club. They came across the bay in Boats to carry us by water to their town. I have seldom witnessed a more brilliant display of these young fellows many of them most respectably dressed — and all heavy [?] with patriotism & intelligence. Our demonstration I gather had men in it to content the heart if not to captivate the Eye than any similar demonstration which I ever attended.[34] We were received at Bantry which we reached with a wet sheet and a flowing sail, by several thousand persons. There we [were] addressed in a very effective manner and after receiving all manner of testimonies of affection from the People I accompanied Mr Shea Lawlor to his home, sat a good good dinner and being excessively tired went to bed almost before the Cloth was removed.

God bless the children.   Ever yours most affect
                                                      W. O'B.

Many little incidents & scenes which I saw need time to extend. These shall be re[served] for the future.

I have extended my tour. I have caught a cold probably from a damp bed.

26. *William Smith O'Brien to Lucy O'Brien (at Dromoland; letter redirected from 78 George's Street, Limerick)*

                                                      [Cork]
                                                      [12 July 1848]

                        [*beginning of letter missing*]

I propose to go today to Dublin by steamer in order to consult with our friends in Dublin. This change of plans has been occasioned by the arrest of Duffy and others. It is rather annoying to me to be compelled so often to change my plans but in the end it may possibly be advantageous.

I wish that I could banish from your mind apprehension, but as I fear that my endeavour would be futile I want only to ask [you] to bear the anxieties of your position with a resolute spirit.

Ask Edward whether the son of Chief Justice Blackburn[35] is drilled at Stachallan [St Columba's College]. I cannot reconcile to myself the transportation of a young boy for saying 'Stand at ease' &c. If he is drilled the fact ought to be known.

Give my love to the dear children & to all at Dromoland. I direct this letter to Limerick uncertain when it may reach you. Address your next to Milland [Westland?] Row — Dublin.

Yrs always most affectly

W.O'B.

27. *Anne Martineau to Mary Lady O'Brien and Ellen (wife of Robert O'Brien)*

Clonmel

21 September [1848]

My dearest Mary & Ellen,

I am sorry to say that I have at the end of the first day only to record that the G-Jury have found two bills against W^m McManus & 2 Farmers & they are all to be tried together which is very annoying to W^m. I was just coming out of the Jail with Robert and Mr Greig[36] when one of the Men said in passing M^rs O'Brien has been sent for Robert & Mr Greig rushed off to secure places in the Courthouse & I waited near to see what happened as Lucy's lodgings were close by. The poor Prisoners came out in a close Van guarded by Police the H Sheriffe a friend of ours walking at their head. As soon as they had passed a quantity of military poured out of a back street & went down another way towards the Court House.

Meantime I slipped back to Mamma's house some distance off with Lucys lodging maid as my escort. There seemed very little movement

& a very small crowd round the Court House, never were a set of people so cowed. Meagher says they are a regular set of cowards.

We have had a leveé all day. The H. Sheriffe is to see Robert [O'Brien], then all sorts of people & finally Lady Osborne also Baron Pennefather[37] nothing can be more exciting than the whole matter of being here, but Mamma seems quite up to it & I do not think will suffer.

She saw W^m at 12 o'clock today & bore it pretty well. Grace went with her. Mr Greig says when put into the Dock with those 3 inferiors he looking so gentlemanlike & particularly well dressed he first flushed & then grew deadly pale & looked very much annoyed, but he has not seen him since. He thought he should be tried *alone* or else with Meagher.

Lucy bore the journey very well wonderfully tho she had an upset or rather a fright & half upset in a car by the band breaking & setting them all down on the ground. M^r & Mrs Greig travelled with them. Lucy cannot *walk* thro' the town at all as she is known & the *poor* prisoners wives follow her. Indeed we are all pretty well stared at. Mamma's carriage collects a regular mob.

I am sick of the Irish people just now. I send you a note for Mrs Sweeny & Mrs Vernon's address *London* & her directions.

Farewell. I wish we were altogether. Ever

Your very affe^ct

Anne

28. *Charlotte, Dowager Lady O'Brien, to Ellen O'Brien*

Clonmel
[24] September 1848

My Dearest Ellen,

I have not written to you since I left Dromoland & yet there is no one I more wish to have near me for few enter into my feeling as you do.

Anne is very kind & a great comfort to me but I cannot venture to speak to her of fears & you know how painful it is to be obliged to be silent. It is better however not to agitate her. She has I am sure deep fears

& anxieties herself and expresses very nice religious sentiments but she does not like to hear any thing contrary to her wishes from others.

I see evidently that the Ladies & Gentlemen who visit here think very badly of Williams case; and Lucy says he is quite prepared for Transportation. Yet he to me seems so calm & his countenance so much more composed than it has appeared for years that I cannot but fancy he has some secret expectation of deliverance in some way or other. Yesterday I went to the Gaol late that I might avoid the dinner hour but found they were late too & just sitting at it so I had an opportunity of seeing Meagher and as he sat opposite to me I could observe his countenance which appeared to me much more marked by strong painful feeling than William's. He is as unlike what I expected from the description given of him as you can well conceive any thing in my mind but boyish looking on the contrary gave me the idea of a most resolute determined man ready for any thing & who would set his face as a flint to accomplish his purpose. I expected to have found him tall and slight & springy, but he is rather stout & thick set — something in shape like Robert Studdert. He said very little while I was there & as soon as he had finished his dinner took up his hat & went away; they have good airy rooms in the part of the Jail used as an Hospital no other rooms near. We went up a short staircase & at the top of it were their two bedrooms & a sitting room. Lucy looked very poorly yesterday & Grace looks ill also, but they do not *appear* cast down. Roberts absence is a great loss to us, but I suppose we shall have him & Henry tomorrow or Tuesday when I hope to have Lucius & Mr. FitzGerald also. Then will be the very anxious period for we do not at present know what plan of defence has been arranged in Dublin. Whatever it may be I still feel that Williams situation is most perilous and that we have great need to prepare our hearts for Submission to the will of God. Nothing else can bring us peace at the last.

As I will not write to Lucius today pray tell him that he had best drive here in the first instance & that he is to enquire for Mr Phelans the Wine Merchants house opposite the Mechanics Institute. It is quite at the end of Anglesea Street.

I expected a parcel from Ballinostor before I left which I have reason to believe went last week to Connolly the Butcher in Ennis & is probably now at Dromoland. Will you try & get it for me & send it here by Lucius? I do not think of any thing else I want & have very little to say but What you know from the papers. I will therefore now say farewell requesting you to give my best love to Mary & the Children and to believe me Dearest Ellen.

Yr very afft Mother
C. O'Brien

I feel much less harried & agitated here than at Dromoland the Seeing William & being in the way of hearing any thing at once is a great comfort to me.

29. *Charlotte, Dowager Lady O'Brien, to William Smith O'Brien*

Dromoland
7 May 1850

My Dear Child,

Your present situation makes me very unhappy but what can be done for you. Your mistaken notions respecting your country's good have brought you into a position I well knew would be deeply painful to you & I really cannot see what is to deliver you from it but the graceful acceptance of any favours the British Government is willing to grant. You were led astray by a party here who were satisfied to receive what they wanted to get by instalments. Why will you not in your private capacity follow O'Connells example & accept the first instalment of good that may be intended for you. While you reject it how can you expect that more will be offered. I know well you never had a thought of trying to escape from Van Diemens land. Why then will you not say so?[38] Why will you not do what every debtor who enjoys the Priveleges of the Queens Bench is obliged to do? Why will you not follow the example of the highest & most honourable prisoners of war who in these very countries enjoyed comparative liberty & comfort when let out on Parole? Will you, can you say that a French officer who continued incarcerated while his companions were visiting in the Country was more noble minded than they because he would not give his Parole? Could you venture to assert that a Debtor who sulkily remained within the iron gratings of the Fleet was more to be esteemed than the men who have visited me in London within the rules of the Queen's Bench under promise not to go into any street not within those rules? Surely it is perfect Childishness to throw away a good within reach because we cannot get all we should like to obtain? Dearest William lay aside this Childishness. Act like a man & make yourself & your family happy by receiving in a kindly spirit & under any promises required the instalment of good however small which may be offered; trusting that in God's own time a larger amount will be given you.

I have read your letters with the greatest pain. I picture you to myself day & night, separated from all those associations with your wife & children which rendered imprisonment in Dublin, & even at Clonmel comparative happiness but I cannot help asking myself, does William, or does he not, see the hand of God in what is now upon him. Dearest William answer the question to yourself. Consider of what importance it is that you should see & know & feel your position with reference to the righteous governor of the world. Until you do your mind never can have rest. You can never pray aright. You can never ask for the things you really need. On the contrary you may be looking for, asking for, & expecting things, which God in mercy to both soul & body may see fit to deny. My dear child consider this subject well. Read your Bible with reference to it. Pray for light & knowledge to understand every part of that Bible aright. Pray for the gifts & graces of the Holy Spirit that every thought & every feeling may be brought into captivity to the will of God. Endeavour to realize the presence of our blessed Immanuel who 'tho He was rich yet for our sakes became poor that we thru His poverty may be made rich.' And may you be enabled so to realize it that the very loneliness of your Prison may be to you a cause for gratitude through the unspeakable enjoyment an ever present God who can be touched with the feeling of our infirmity will bring to your Soul. You may be supported for a while by Stoical or wounded feelings, but you never can be partaker of that Peace which passeth all understanding until you look to the Lord Jes[us] Christ with singleness & simplicity of mind & tr[ust] in Him for the supply of all your wants.

To Him & to the word of His Grace do I now commend you. May you find Him a very present help in this time of trouble. And may you so know him & Love Him as to be able under the severest trials to rejoice in Him with joy unspeakable & full of Glory.

Believe me my dear child with all a Mothers Sympathy & tender feeling for one who was brought up in ease & comfort & with the prospect of every enjoyment this life could afford your most truely affectionate

Mother
C. O'Brien

I say nothing of Lucy
and your dear children you hear
from them frequently —

30. *William Smith O'Brien to Lucy O'Brien (at Cahirmoyle; letter arrived in November 1852)*

New Norfolk
27 June 1852

My Darling Wife,

After long long expectation I have received from you two most cheering letters one dated Jan^r 3. the other Jan^r 24, with enclosures from Lucy and Edward. Altogether I have not been in such good spirits since I arrived in this colony as today the same post has brought me remittances from Robert O'B £50 (5 Janry) and £130 29 Janry which will enable me to discharge all outstanding pecuniary engagements in this colony, whilst by the same post I have also received a letter from Mr Lapham informing me that he has been appointed police magistrate in Victoria (Port Philip) at a salary of upwards of £400 per ann. This last piece of intelligence is more welcome to me than would be the receipt of £1000. If he lives for 10 or 15 years he will be enabled to provide for his family under very advantageous circumstances & I shall be spared what would otherwise be a perpetual occasion of anxiety.[39]

I am also beginning to hope something from the movement in America in favor of the Irish Exiles. Though I expect nothing from the magnanimity of England I think it possible that something may be extracted from her calculating selfishness & her apprehensions. At present if not threatened with invasion she is at least without a friend on the Continent and she will not if she is wise offend public feeling in America by refusing a request which costs her nothing to grant.[40] If we were inclined for mischief we should be much more dangerous here than we could be at home and for myself I will not promise to exercise throughout the remainder of my life the same forbearance & self control which I have exercised during my residence in Australia in case she refuses to restore me to my native land. If an unconditional amnesty were granted to all the Irish Exiles & refugees I should feel myself under a moral obligation to abstain from smiting with the arm which had been unbound even by a foe, but anything short of a general amnesty will obtain no thanks from me. I will wait patiently until the chapter of accidents brings a change of circumstances, or until death affords a not unwelcome relief from my present sufferings.

I trust that I shall soon cease to apply to myself the word 'suffering'. Indeed it seems very ungrateful on my part to apply it to myself when I remember how much I have to console me. Is any one more blest in his children than I am — in his wife — in his relations? Have I not been the object of affectionate solicitude to millions who can even under reverses of the least glorious kind appreciate the purity of my motives and the earnestness of my endeavours for the welfare of my country & of mankind? Far from repining I ought to exult — I do not exult because I feel my own imperfections more strongly than others can feel them, but I trust that I am deeply grateful for the many mercies still vouchsafed to me.

Do not make any apologies about your disposition to tell me Everything that concerns the children. What can you say that will interest me half so much. Your accounts of them are to me most heart consoling. Dear Edward how much pride and comfort do I feel in looking forward to the time when he will assume the character of protector of all who are dear to me. You must endeavour to impress upon his mind that if it please God to spare his life I look to him to supply my place as father to a family bereaved of their parent. I am sorry to find that you have set your face against his entering Trinity College Dublin during the present year. As for Mr Williams I have not the least confidence in his judgmt. I can never forget that he threatened Edward with a flogging an insult which would have induced me to remove him at once from St. Columba if I had been in Ireland. All the arguments which may be urged in favor of an English university education were equally applicable nay much more applicable with regard to his education at school. Nevertheless I fought against my own prejudices tried the experiment of an Irish school and have never ceased to congratulate myself both on my own account and on that of my country that I was enabled to overcome my prejudices against an Irish school education. I know what Cambridge is as well as Mr Williams.[41] I know that I learnt there much that was evil and little that was good. If therefore my opinion is considered of any importance in regard to the Education of my children I have to repeat my wish that Edward should go to Trinity College Dublin at the Earliest possible moment. Of course I wish that every possible precaution should be taken to prevent him from falling into bad associations of any kind, but I consider that a boy who has relatives & friends residing in Dublin is infinitely less in danger of getting into bad associations at Trin Coll— Dublin than at Cambridge or Oxford. There is some danger lest he should be led to fritter away his time in general society but if he be determined to read steadily for University honors the emulation of academical rivalry will act as a counter impulse to the attractions of society.

You may show this letter to Edward. I have always treated him & shall continue to treat him not as a mere child but as a friend. He will

be fully capable of appreciating my feelings. I have again
hope that Robert Gabbett [Vicar of Shanagolden] ·
ics with him for two or three months before he g<
I will write to Robert G. to thank him for his kindi.
teach Lucius. I consider that the proposal is most advantag
must consent to receive payment on the same terms as if he wer
Stranger. Remember that if I continue in Australia I am desirous that
Edward should pay me a visit before he begins to practise law in Dublin
and also that he should spend at least six months on the Continent of
Europe. If you delay his education at the university this cannot be
effected without interfering with his professional pursuits. I consider it
of *paramount* importance that he should be thoroughly versed in the law
& in the practice of the Courts. It is possible that he may have to defend
his own inheritance and he should be prepared either for the alternative of securing it or of rendering [?] himself independent of it.

I am greatly pleased with the composition of Lucy's last letter but
not with the handwriting. Though Miss Sharman wrote a good hand
herself she does not seem to have been successful in teaching Lucy to
write. I have no doubt however that she will write well bye & bye. How
much I long to see the dear little ones. I know the dispositions & characters of the Elder but what can I know of Murrough[42] except through
your representation. It is truly satisfactory to find that he is so promising a child. Would to God that I could see them all again!

I am much happier here than I was last year at the Red Rock. I
occupy myself with my studies & when I want a little change I go to
visit some of the kind friends who have endeavoured to make a *home*
for me in this country. Among this number is *not* Archdeacon Marriott and it mortifies me not a little to find that my mother writes to
him as to a 'friend of the family.' I have been here six months since my
return during which time he has not once asked me even to take a cup
of tea in his house. His brother in law [William Sharland] a lowbred
upstart is the great man of the village and a friend of the Governor,
Sir Wm. Denison. From him I did not expect to receive any atten-
tions but from Archdeacon Marriott[43] I might have expected a differ-

ent feeling. Upon the whole I am not at all sorry that I am not on terms of intimate acquaintance with him for he bears the character of a cold hearted mean, selfish creature and from the hour of my arrival in this colony to the present moment I never have heard a single person of any description give him a good word, but I confess that it annoys me much to find my mother corresponding with such a person & not only corresponding but suggesting surveillance respecting my religious principles &c. Archdeacon Marriot belongs to what is called the Romanising party of the Church of England Clergymen in this Colony. This party with the Bishop at their head have been resorting of late to a proscription which is wholly unjustifiable of the Clergy who approach in opinion nearest to the religious convictions of my mother. It really seems almost absurd therefore that my mother should write to Archdeacon Marriott about my Romanising tendencies. From the Catholic clergy in this colony I have received the utmost possible kindness. I love and Esteem many Roman Catholics and upon the whole I consider the Catholics more humbly pious than t[he] Protestants but I am not disposed to surrender [my r]ight of private judgment either to the Bishop of Tasmania or to the Pope. I do not wish to annoy my mother about such subjects or indeed about any thing. I therefore will not trust myself to write to her but shall feel much obliged if you will prevent her from writing any more to Archdeacon Marriott about me.

I am greatly grieved to hear that [dear Mrs] Hall has lost her husband and also Elliot Warburton has perished in the Amazon. I can scarcely tell you how much pleased I was by her visit which Anne Hall paid me when I was in Prison. My regard for those whom I have once loved never changes by Efflux of time, though it may change from a change of feeling upon their part. I do not know whether this is what ought properly be called Constancy. If this be constancy I am the most constant of men. If constancy mean but Love for one alone I fear that I cannot claim the title. Of this however be assured dearest wife that in all my wanderings through this world of care I have never seen any one who so entirely deserves and possesses my affection esteem and gratitude as my incomparable Lucy. It rejoices me to hear that Lucy's father is so well and strong. The day of his departing must soon arrive but surely it is a great blessing that his spirits and his health have been retained to so advanced an age. As for Lucy's mother (shall I not also call her my dearest mother?) I will not augur any premature loss. I hope again to see her before we die.[44] Tell her that with the utmost sincerity I can say that I have known few very few persons for whom I entertain such an affectionate regard as that which I feel for the mother of my incomparable wife. I cannot call to mind one single occasion upon which she ever wounded my feelings. This is perhaps more than I can say for any other human being now alive with whom I have been on terms of intimacy.

> Ever yr devoted husband
> William S. O'Brien

31. *William Smith O'Brien to Lucy O'Brien*

> New Norfolk, Van Diemen's Land
> 17 October 1852

My dearest Wife,

Again another birth day has arrived and I am still 'all alone' — alone! alone!

> 'What is the worst of ills that wait an age?
> To be alone on earth as I am now!'—

Never Mind! I must keep up my spirits. I live on from day to day — from week to week and I suppose I shall continue to do so from year to year without being able to Form any plan of life or to engage in any occupation that can interest me — or to enjoy the society of any whom I can love. Never mind! There is no day so long but that it will have an end and whether that end came soon or twenty years hence is comparatively of little importance when time is considered in relation to eternity. I am often astonished at the calm tranquil patience with which my restless spirit bears the sort of life which I now lead. When I was at the

Red Rock indeed I was very unhappy, but since my return to New Norfolk I have continued to live on from day to day without sinking into dejection. Indeed I have so much cause for thankfulness still remaining that I should be very ungrateful if I were to repine.

I send this note in company with the Journal which will I trust reach you with the same regularity as former portions. I hope that you have copied what I have already sent. I fancy that after I am dead and gone this journal will at some future time be interesting to the public and it would ease my mind much if I could persuade myself that in now compiling it for your gratification I am at the same time making a provision for my younger children which will compensate them for the loss sustained through the *robbery* inflicted upon them by the English Insurance Company.[45] If you copy only one page each day you will soon get through the whole journal. You ought to copy it on one page only of each leaf leaving the other blank so that it might at once be put into the hands of the printer in case of my death.

I am beginning again to await with impatience the receipt of a letter from you as about a month has elapsed since I last received one. During this interval I have written to you, to Grace, to Lucius, to Henry, to Charles Harris and to Robert.

[*remainder missing*]

32. *Lucy O'Brien to William Smith O'Brien*

[Cahirmoyle]
29 January [1854]

My dear William,

We are still uncertain as to the truth of the report of your escape[46] but it will not do to leave you with out letters & money. Robert has therefore resolved to send your money under cover to Mr Carter to be returned if you have left the Colony. I do not believe the report as Kate has received a paper from you of the 24th of September the latest letter was one to Anne of the 2nd of September & I have *since* received letters enclosed to the children of the 14th of August. The Post is terribly irregular but in the end I believe we receive all the letters. I have been very anxious as you may guess ever since we heard this report, not knowing whether it would be best or not. We all felt that *you could* not give even a reason to have yourself spoken of as a breaker of parole but we do not know whether it would be well to have you escape or wait quietly in hopes of a pardon which will permit you to return *home*. In case you should make yr escape I *entreat you as you love your children* to avoid making speeches in America or in any way identifying your self with the party who are for ever abusing England. It would be such a serious injury to your young people if you wish them to live in Ireland & would place all your family in such a painful position. I am amazed at the virulent tone of Meagher's speeches except that one knows his vanity is so great & he speaks for applause. Mr. Mitchell can never astonish one after the articles he wrote in 47 & 48.

I had a visit on the 18th from a Mr. Smythe. He was so kind as to remember how much I should like to speak to a person who had seen you & on the whole I found his visit a very pleasant one as he told me you looked well & are tolerably comfortably situated. I was fortunately in Limerick which saved him the trouble of the drive out here. We had a long chat about you Australia & America. He has imbibed in a wonderful degree American views on the slavery question & quite seeks to justify it. I wonder how a man feeling as Meagher once did can be acquiescent even by silence, in such a crime but Mr. Smythe says he would lose his warmest friends if he mentioned the subject though he denies that he would be Lynched. I think Mr Smythe did not at all approve of your giving away copies of Uncle Tom's Cabin. I greatly enjoyed talking with one who had lately seen you & much wish he had seen the boys as he said he meant to write to you.[47]

Edward & Lucius went on the morning of the 18th to St. Columba & Willie to his school. He was at home for the Xmas as Anne could not conveniently have him this winter[48] — He enjoyed himself immensely poor fellow but I confess I much prefer his not coming home at Christmas it is such a *very* anxious thing crossing at this season. He went over in a storm. Had I guessed he was out in it I sh^d have been very miserable but I am thankful he is again safe at school as it continues to blow great guns. One Emigrant vessel to Australia was lost either the night he crossed or the next one. It was lost outside Kingstown Harbour[49] & more than 400 people have perished, principally German & Irish. Just as we were leaving home for Limerick Edward received a letter from the Warden telling him that he had gained the verse composition prize for which he had worked very hard & which was competed for by the *four* Royal Irish schools Radley in England of which Sewell is warden & Glenalmond in Scotland of which Wordsworth is head, The boys in both being much Edward's seniors. I send you a paper with the account & am told there is an article in the *Standard* which speaks most highly of your boy. You will be gratified by his ability & success, dear boy his first thought was that it would cheer you to know that he has not forgotten your instructions & maxims. Need I tell you that I am gratified but how infinitely more so by all. He is besides so humble, obedient & affte.

He has so entirely conquered his naturally proud spirit that he frankly says he is wrong & sorry. This is much for one who as a *very little* child never would *cry* except from passion. You will probably see in the papers all the unpleasant correspondance about the Warden. I for one am indifferent as to his signature of the protest but I avow I am grieved by the want of straightforwardness evinced in his letters. The College has been much injured by the business. The Primate having withdrawn his support & most people looking on Mr Wms as a Jesuit in disguise. We are however quite satisfied with the moral & religious training of our boys & have sent them back.[50] I do not know where you could find nicer lads than St. Columba Members so unlike the usual run of school boys. Lucius is the dearest & most attractive of boys not clever perhaps but so aimiable & gentlemanly. Edward took Don[agh] in hands when he was at home & has brightened him up astonishingly. I am told he is clever but he is very silent & undemonstrative growing very tall & will end by being good looking as he has a *splendid* white forehead & a very sweet smile. Edward has imbued Lucy with a strong desire to learn Latin & Greek. She has commenced the former & gives up ½ an hour daily to her

Latin Grammar & writes an exercise which she means to make Robert correct for her. She is certainly very clever & wonderfully persevering but what is far better she is *now* good tempered gentle & aff^te. We are indeed greatly blessed in our children. I am very lonely Having sent Lucy into Limerick to my mother for a month. There is a german master in the town & I thought it a pity not to let her have some lessons as she is so desirous to improve. She is also to attend the School of Design & take lessons in dancing. I trust she will enjoy herself & not be troublesome. I know I miss her *sorely*. I never thought I should have felt it so much but she is so useful to me & such a nice little companion. I must change my governess & am anxiously looking out for an Irish Lady but it is difficult to find a person *fitted to* instruct Lucy & yet willing to accept a small salary. Miss Monk is a kind good woman but not capable of helping your little girl as I could wish. Edward & Charley completed their 17th & 5th years last Tuesday. Charley is a fine fellow in all respects, one you would enjoy. The mother & all the family at Dromoland are well. Ellen not worse than usual but I do not doubt that she will be very much better & happier too in her new house as it is warm & sunny & she can do as she likes. Besides being *at home* is some thing. Lucius's girls are rapidly growing up. July is almost 11 & looks more than that age. I trust Lucius will not marry again but Grace & Robert evidently think he will.[51] It wd be very unpleasant to the girls I don't fancy step mothers. Frank Fitzgerald of Adelphi died last week quite suddenly I am told. I wonder what effect it will have on Mr. Wm Fitzs property but I have heard nothing about it save from common report.

Whilst I am writing I am brought in the post with your letter of October the 1st setting at rest the story of your escape. I wonder how people can be so unfeeling as to tell lies which cause an entire family so much anxiety. We have been so very uneasy at not hearing from America supposing you had really gone & fearing that you might still be a wanderer. If you do change your mind & try the chance I hope you will arrange for some one to let us hear at once & write the moment you are any where else. Also that you will forbear all attacks on England. If you were indeed a free man & were quite still it might bring you the quicker to Ireland. From all I can learn of other lands none are so free as this & in none other I am sure can you be really happy. I[t] seems to me that the country is improving tho' prices are enormously high just now in consequence of this [Crimean] war panic. It is curious how very many of your plans for the improvement of the country are being carried out. We want however that which no government can give or withhold, i.e. *Truth & Union*.

All promise much & perform *nothing* & abuse one another unsparingly. As to what you say of the De Veres I agree with you that they are a highly intellectual & aimiable family but Currah House when inhabited which is very rarely is made so unpleasant to Ellen[52] even by the intolerable *bigotry* of the Perverts that even she has ceased to be there except to see her mother & the old Lady's home is evidently far from a happy one, besides as I told you before they were *very marked* in their coldness *to your wife* on my return home & never even called on me tho' they then went every where. I certainly do not now wish to intrude on them. However I believe they are not likely to want me. You cannot conceive anything like the fanaticism of men like Wm Monsell.[53] It is to me perfectly wonderful. Do not trouble yourself about money matters. I only suggested about Lucy in case you find a *nugget* &c but I am sure not one of the children would wish you to be deprived of the *smallest* comfort for their indulgence much less Edward or Lucy. We only wish we could contribute to your comforts. As to this Income tax people have taken it quietly as it is put on in exchange for one which pressed more heavily. As to any struggle being made by the so called Irish party[54] there are *so few* if any honest [men] that they can do nothing but it is supposed there will be a tremendous struggle between parties before Easter. I get old papers from your mother & my brother Joe between them I gain old *information* but it is well enough for me — I do not remember any thing more to tell you just now but perhaps I may hear of something tomorrow before I close this. We expect my sister Alice in Europe next spring. She has two little girls & is again in that way not to be confined until July. I long much to see her again. Her husband [John Surtees Stockley, RA] does not return until Autumn. I believe he is a good kind man & that she is happy which is much to counter balance the unpleasantness of the connection. I often fear she will find home unpleasant. In Canada she was most kindly treated by all classes. William is married. His wife is very pleasing & sensible. I told you I met her at my mothers before she thought of visiting India — He was able to make a good provision for her & any bairns — Robert as usual. Mr. Latouche has left him for which Robert does not lament. How much you would enjoy the vicarage. I am told that Cahircon has been taken (under the Courts) by a young Mr. Wesby he has lately married Miss Blackbourne. It will be a very good thing if true. William Waller's eldest son Bolton is dead very suddenly he was a fine young man. John the present eldest is a parson aimiable & good but very delicate. Old Mr. Waller of Shannon Grove has also gone. Shannon Grove is now inhabited by a Mr. Hewson of Askeaton. The Russells are doing much in that town & growing Prince Merchants. How shocked you will be at so many sheets but were I to cross you never read. This paper is so thin & I respect your eyes. Mine are not so good as they have been.

I forgot to say that the Ornithorhynchus[55] has never been received by us. Mr. Thompson sent me your journal but has not come over himself perhaps he *will*. What is native *Bread* is vegetable, *animal* or mineral & how used &c. *Tell us* I never heard of it before. I hope the kangaroo rat[56] is well & with you.

Monday 30th There are no letters for me by this days post.

The Papers contained the account of a terrible shipwreck off Lambay Island near Dublin. More than 400 people lost. Some accounts say 455 — Emigrants bound for Melbourne from Liverpool. Many Irish. Indeed mostly so. The prevailing winds this winter have been East & S.E. but last night & the night before [there had] been a great storm from the West.

Good bye my dear husband. God bless you & give you all the comfort you can have in your exile.

Your affect wife
Lucy C. O'Brien

33. William Smith O'Brien to Lucy O'Brien

New Norfolk
28 June 1854

My Darling Wife,

Yesterday I received the 'Conditional Pardon' in due form without note or comment. I was rather afraid that I should be called upon to make application for it in some form or other — and as I had firmly resolved not to say or write or do any thing which could be interpreted as a confession on my part that I consider myself a 'criminal' in regard of the transactions of 1848. I had made up my mind that not withstanding the demonstrations made in the House of Commons I should be left to die in VD Land *alone*. I now rejoice to find that I can at all events get near home and for a time at least a residence on the Continent will be agreeable rather than otherwise, but I am still left without a home, a wanderer on the Face of the Earth. I have not lost a day in setting out on my journey. I have left Richmond I trust for Ever. The two months which I spent there were passed very agreeably considering. I am here now to take leave of my friends in this district. Next week I return to Hobart Town in order to receive an address which has been got up there. Afterwards I go for a similar reason to Launceston. Thence I intend to proceed to Melbourne. If I have time & find that the Journey will not be too Expensive I will go for a few days to Sydney[57] & return by the overland mail.

I have received your letter of 13th March by which I am happy to learn that Donagh & Charles have got over their illness — also a letter from Robert enclosing an order for £100, arrived very seasonably and a few lines from my brother Henry. I need not tell you that I am in excellent spirits, though I am unable to tell you which is the next spot in the world from which I shall write to you, still less when we shall meet.

With affect love to all friends who are entitled to such love.

Ever your most attached
William S. O'Brien

34. *Lucy O'Brien to William Smith O'Brien*

Cahirmoyle
25 November [1854]

My dearest William,

I have just received your Paris letter of the 21st of November & am now anxiously expecting one from Brussells with some decided advice as to our movements. If you had sent to the Poste restante at Malta you would I suppose have received Robert's letter & mine which would have determined your plans in a great measure. I also wrote both to Paris & Brussells & hope you have received both or one of my letters. This letter I send on chance of your going to the Post at the latter place. If I hear from you *within the next week* with a direction as to where you are to be found Edward will start off *at once* to join you. I will write as soon as I can tell you the day he goes & to what port. He is so desirous to see you that I could not object to his immediate journey as he must be in Dublin by Xmas to read for his January examination as our friends all say it would be a loss to him to drop it & I think it a sad pity to idle him, unless *necessary*.

As to our journey I should much prefer travelling *without* any protector. I am an old woman now & in our country Venus might move unattended, if she did get into passions every one is civil & attentive. I should certainly like to have the pleasure of first meeting you & with my boy but I could never move in less than a fortnight & it would then be impossible for Ed. to go before Janry.

I should *extremely* dislike to go without a governess abroad. Indeed I think it will *be far better* to do without masters if necessary than without one & having taken very great trouble to procure such an Irish lady as I now have I trust you will not deprive Lucy of the great advantage of her society. She is a lady in every respect & a very good pleasing woman. Your mother pays £40 out of £50 of her salary & Miss D'Arcy will not object I am certain to any arrangement we may think it desirable to make as to sharing her bedroom or making it into a school room &c &c. Ed will tell you more than I can write & I am sure you would not desire our dear little girl to go to school abroad I *certainly* should not. As to a Maid I will not take one if you think I had better wait *until* we arrive in — as the Maid who has been with us for 4 years may not accompany us her husband does not wish it. I am very sorry as she would have been invaluable to us.

Robert & I looked over our affairs some days since & we came to the conclusion that it would be unwise to sell the *very little* furniture we have as there are no bidders in this country. Besides this *I am* sure if you are quite *quiet* & *silent* you will be allowed home ere long say in a year or so perhaps less. I think it would be vain to seek for a good tenant without the ground & I should much regret to have the place spoilt. Ed likes it much & so do all the children as well as myself. I therefore wish to leave a woman *in* the House & a man to look after the place. This will not cost us over £30 a year & will enable us to return when we please.

Our income after *all* deductions for boys &c &c must not be calculated as more than £500 per ann for our personal expenses. At least we should not reckon on drawing more than it *in money* for the present as there are many expenses which will be all explained by the statements I will take you.

I fancy if we are to reside in Brussells or elsewhere it will be best to take 'appartemens garines' — have our dinner from traiteurs &c, but Kate will write all this to you. I should much like to send Don after Xmas to St C[olumba's], if possible this would reduce our family to *three* [underlined twice] bedrooms & a salon if Miss D's room was large enough for a sitting room, but all this will do when we meet to talk over it. You will I know be very kind & friendly to Miss D'Arcy. You always are so & she is every way worthy of being treated as a friend. We are all well thank God & happy in the thoughts of meeting you, but I am *very nervous* & quite afraid you will be put out by such a family. You never have had as yet any charge of them you know & now they are a *troop*.

I forgot to tell you that we i.e. *R & I* think it quite out of the question keeping up two homes so you must become the father & *Head* [underlined twice] of a family. I have always spoken unreservedly to E^d on all subjects so you may treat him as a reasonable being & a right feeling one. My pen is quite stiff in my hand, it is so cold today I can *scarce* write. Very cold for our journey but what must it be to the poor soldiers in the Crimea. We all think a great deal of them. There is scarce a house in which there are not anxious hearts. I cannot forgive the sort of half triumphant way in which the *Nation* speaks of our loss of troops & the suffering of our men as if we were not all equally concerned. It is shocking bad feeling I must think. I feel deeply for the Russians but how much more for our own poor men.

Lucius & all at Dromoland are getting on nicely. I believe Lady O'Brien is an aimiable cheerful person & has much tact.

Willy's vacation will coincide in or about the 17th, Lucius on the 20th of next month. Am I to *wait* for them or let them take their chance as to travelling?

Say all you wish me to do. I have been desired not to take house linen or books &c. Plate we have next to none indeed what I use is my Mother's so is the harness of my car &c &c. Never mind we shall be rich in content I trust. Am I to take *books* I fear they would be heavy unless we *settled* somewhere & as I have *resolved* to come over to see my Mother every year D.V. I could at any time bring what you require. Have you read Macaulay's Essays if not I think they would please you.

I send you some violets from Charley, pleasant to think they will not have lost their perfume by the length of the journey.

God bless you my dear William.

Write as soon & as fully as you can.

I must pay Miss D'Arcy a quarters salary if I dismiss her but I know she will not be an hour disengaged.

Your very affect wife
Lucy C. O'Brien

Robert had sent the £100 to P. & B. for you & has desired your drafts to be honored to the Amount of £200 more but he could not *lodge* more or I should have no money to take me or with me. He is prepared to give me £200 to take with me.

Write to me	Robert O'Briens
the days the	address is
London vessel	*Old Church*
leaves for *Ostend*	Circular road
It is a shorter	*Limerick.*
passage.	

35. *William Smith O'Brien to Lucy Josephine O'Brien (daughter) (at Cahirmoyle)*

Paris

3 November 1855

My Dearest Lucy,

I send you a little song which I bought at a stall for two pence. It has no great merit but it will prove that I thought of you when I was buying it. I send also a *centime* for your collection of coins which will prove that I thought of you at another time. I have a shirt too *unmarked* which will make me think of you whenever I put it on. Now my dearest daughter I hope that whilst you are [at] Cahirmoyle you will learn all sorts of *domestic industry*. Whilst you had masters at Bruxelles for whom you required time to prepare your exercises I was unwilling to press you too much to give up your time to homely labours, but at Cahirmoyle you have not the same reasons for neglecting this branch of *Education*, the most important to which a young woman can apply herself. Adele will be able to teach you all that is necessary for cutting out clothes and I confess that it would give me the greatest pleasure to hear that you make all your own clothes as well as some for Murrough. I do not wish you to give up the piano, nor even to abstain from learning Latin but I consider that a woman's *duties* are more important than a lady's accomplishments and still more important than the attainment of those branches of knowledge which are usually supposed to belong exclusively to the male sex. You will have ample time for acquiring proficiency in both departments.

I hope that you will continue to practice drawing in all its branches, sketching from nature as well as copying from pictures. You have a decided talent for drawing and if you take pains to cultivate it you may perhaps acquire such proficiency as would enable you to earn a livelihood by it in case you should hereafter become dependent upon your own exertions for an honorable and independent subsistence. How many changes of social position have I seen during the short space of twenty-five years among persons who entered life with expectations of fortune far less precarious than those which you inherit. I wish *all* my children to acquire that sense of independence which arises from feeling that if matters 'come to the worst' they can acquire by their own talents and industry a decent livelihood. I regret to find that this sort of language is not acceptable in my household but nevertheless it is my duty to hold of it and I shall continue to urge it until I see that my wishes in this respect are fully accomplished. Then further preaching on the subject will be unnecessary.

I have been in Paris just one week and have found my life here much less agreeable than that spent at Brusselles, although Paris is said to be the centre [of] society and excitement. It is true the weather has been most excessively dismal. Except for a few hours there has been a constant drizzle of rain and as my spirits depend much upon the sun I do not expect to recover them until I get into the warmer and sunnier regions of the south. I was in hopes that Edward would have arrived here yesterday. I w[ish for] his society very much.

I hope that you will write to me occasionally (that is very often) a few lines and take great pains with your penmanship.

The exhibition of pictures is I think very fine and I much wish that you could see it but I do not find in it many masterpieces of the highest order of excellence. There is an immense quantity of good pictures but few of supereminent merit.

Give my love to the children collectively and separately. They will miss me sometimes. Tell them that I hope I shall find as much reason to praise them when we meet next as when I was at Bruxelles.

I remain
Your affect father
William S. O'Brien

[*Postscript*]

November 7 1855

My Dearest Wife,

Since that above was written Edward and Charles Harris[58] have arrived. Nothing untoward has occurred. We propose to proceed towards Lyons on next Friday or Saturday. Send to Lyons *poste restante* any letters which you may write within the next week — say before the 15th. I suppose that we shall leave Lyons before the 18th. The weather has been very disageeable during the whole of our stay at Paris.

I will write to you again soon. Enclosed is a memorandum respecting the studies of the boys. Do not allow it to be lost.

Yours ever most affect
W.S.O'B.

36. *Lucy O'Brien to William Smith O'Brien*

Kilkee
[10 May 1856]

My dearest Husband,

You are a *free man* to return when you please thank God. I have just received a *line* from Mother announcing that you have received a *Free Pardon* no mistake. I dare say you know it by this time yourself by Telegraph but I spend the 1/1d on the news. My very best love to my boy. May we all meet in happiness Amen.

Your very affect wife
Lucy C. O'Brien

Brighton House
Kilkee

Why do you or Ned not write?

[*Postscipt*]

Saturday May 10th

Dearest Papa,

I am so delighted to think that you may come home to us all. We only heard today. Thank God for the good news. Give my love to Edward and believe me ever dearest Papa your most loving child

Lucy J. O'Brien

Hope to see you very soon at home.

37. *Extract from Journal of an Excursion made during the months of August and September 1861 by William Smith O'Brien*

On the twenty seventh of July 1861 I left Cahirmoyle in search of repose of mind. It is seldom that a traveller undertakes a tour on the continent from such a motive, but I have during several months been so much depressed by the sorrow of a domestic calamity — the greatest that I could sustain; and at the same time I have been so much harassed by anxieties connected with my property that even the excitement incidental to foreign travel will be comparative repose, if I can discharge from my mind the reflections by which it has been recently tortured. The commencement of my journey has been auspicious; who can foresee what will be its end.

38. *William Smith O'Brien to Rev. John Gwynn (husband of Lucy Josephine and Warden of St Columba's College)*

Killiney
22 February 1862

My dear Mr Gwynne,

I am much obliged to you for having sent the boys here. Their presence here has occasioned a most pleasurable excitement in our little circle. I will send them back on Monday afternoon if they be fit for travel. All the family except myself are barking from colds. As for me I thought at one time that 'the rascals' had 'finished me up' for I perceived some admonitory symptoms in the region of my heart which reminded me that I ought to prepare for my latter end, but I am now inclined to believe that I am reserved by the good or the evil spirit to whose care I have been committed for some further adventures which may startle the world. I am afraid that I must end my days by exclaiming

> Sors mea principiis erat irrequieta pigetque
> Actorum sine fine mihi, sine honore, laborum.[59]

I have to thank you also for your 'modified' congratulations. I can scarcely understand the glee which I am greeted by some of my acquaintances, as if it were a matter of congratulations to be turned out of the home in which one had hoped to spend his old age by a base conspiracy got up amongst those who had been trusted as friends. I wonder how his Lordship (soidisant — according to the Athenaeum) would like to be turned out of Dromoland by me in case I had undertaken to protect his estate for him and his family during a crisis in which my intervention might have secured its preservation. I trust however that in the end I shall concur with you in believing that it is possible for a man to be happy when enfranchised from the cares of an estate, and consoled by the receipt of £2000 per annum. When I was convicted of High Treason in 1848 Revd Mr Whiteside by way of amusing me in the Queens Bench gave me a Greek quotation similar to that which you have sent:

> αμεινον το ημισυ του παντοσ
> Better the half than the whole

Whereupon I wrote impromptu

> Better to love the half of life
> than to spend the whole in ceaseless strife.

I have no similar distich for you, but I have not forgotten the old proverb

> 'Half a loaf is better than no bread'.

Yet, μα τουσ θεουσ αθανατουσ, By the immortal gods!

I would not in the day of the hearing of the Chancery [suit] have thrown a pin into the scale to determine the Chancellor's judgement one way or the other. So little am I disposed, *on my own account*, to exult in the recent decision. Still more certain is it that I would not have allowed my three eldest children to act upon Mr Greig's suggestion — to reconvey to me their shares if the Chancellor's decision had been adverse to the family settlement. I would have rather gone forth as a pilgrim wrapped up in my virtue which is rather an equivocal possession in my case. I would have cried

Mea virtute me involvo probamque pauperiem sine dote quaero.[60]

I am inclined however to hope, though upon this point I am by no means certain, that the present arrangement is one which will be more conducive to the happiness of my family than the Heptarchy would have been.

Forgive me for writing on these scraps of paper. I have come to the end of my ream of presentable paper. Yours very sincerely,

W.S.O'B.

39. *Lucy Gwynn to William Smith O'Brien*

St Columba's College
21 May [1863]

My dearest Papa,

I hope you received a letter written to Berlin & that this will find you at Bruxelles where a despatch from Charlotte already waits you. —

I want to tell you of a little change of plans — as to our summer movements. The measles have made such havoc in the school. 20 boys being ill, though all now are on the mend.[61] That John thinks it wise to break up some time earlier than usual this year as the sick boys wd. not be well enough for work again this half. There will be no exams as the most promising boys old and young wd lose their chances of prizes and St Columba's day fete too is an impossibility, as people wd fear infection & there could be no music. The holidays begin on the 6th of June, and as we must go to the north, during the summer, it will be better to do so at once, & thus make sure of being at Cahirmoyle in July when you will be there, so that we shall all meet there, please God, before long. I fear we shall miss you on your way through Dublin, but perhaps you may stay some time in England so that our going south w^d be about the same time. Aunt Grace has been with us for the last few days & will stay a little longer. It is a great pleasure having her here, especially as she seems to enjoy herself, & likes my husband much. She will probably be in London when you return from abroad staying at Gold's house in Park Street. Uncle C[harles] & Aunt K[ate] at Bremhaven [Germany?], the Martineaus either in London or at their new living near Dover. Lucius is in College, and was a good deal better, when last we saw him, very much taken up with cricket, the rest of the party except Don at Cahirmoyle.

We have had a colonial bishop, him of the Orange River States[62] — if you know where they are — staying here. He has been just appointed & goes out as first bishop to his diocese in July. He had been a tutor here in Mr Williams time [and] gave an interesting lecture, about his part of the world. No other news in our quiet life. The weather has been singularly disagreeable lately. Edward and I drove to the place which we thought might suit you but I fear it scarcely would as though the house seems good and there is land about it and rather a nice neighbourhood, it is not pretty enough to take your fancy and besides is a long way from a railway. Please write here — when you are likely to be in Ireland

                                & believe me
                          Y^r most affte daughter
                                Lucy Gwynn

My love to Auguste Potter

40. *William Smith O'Brien to Charlotte Grace O'Brien (daughter)*

Shelbourne Hotel, Dublin
10 February 1864

My Dearest Charlotte,

I have been unwell since Saturday (midday) and having spent the greater part of my time alone have been in rather low spirits.

I have been reluctant to write to you on this subject because I do not wish to diminish your enjoyment of yr visit to your sister, but as it is your duty to attend to me in case of illness I shall hope that you will come and stay with me until I shall be reestablished in health.

I am disposed to think that my remedy will be found in removal from Dublin as the air does not agree with my throat and I am desirous to consult your wishes as to our next move.

I have not consulted a doctor so that I cannot tell you the name of my indisposition but I believe it to be a threatening of *bronchitis*; I suffer occasionally from terrible oppression of an asthmatic kind and to avoid a return of this tendency which was incurred by going out on Monday for a few hours I have remained in the house yesterday and today.

Your affectionate father,
William S. O'Brien

Notes to Introduction

1   Bracketed numbers refer to the subsequent documents.
2   Sir Edward O'Brien to Charlotte Lady O'Brien, 29 July [?] 1808: NLI, Inchiquin Papers, MS 2961.
3   Grania O'Brien, *These My Friends and Forebears: The O'Briens of Dromoland*, (Whitegate, Co. Clare, 1991), pp. 82, 106.
4   W. S O'Brien to Lady O'Brien, 18 Mar. 1819: NLI, Smith O'Brien Papers, MS 8655 (2).
5   W. S. O'Brien to Sir Edward and Lady O'Brien, Saturday 18 [Mar. or Nov.] 1820: ibid.
6   Lucy O'Brien to W. S. O'Brien, 29 Mar. [1841?]: ibid., MS 8654.
7   Richard Davis *et al.* (eds), '*To Solitude Consigned': The Tasmanian Journal of William Smith O'Brien, 1849–53* (Sydney, 1995).
8   W. S. O'Brien to Lucy O'Brien, 19 Feb. 1853: NLI, Smith O'Brien Papers, MS 8653 (29), Reel 17.
9   Stephen Gwynn, *Experiences of a Literary Man* (London, 1926), p. 17.
10 The inscription on Smith O'Brien's statue in O'Connell Street, Dublin, incorrectly gives his date of death as 16 June 1864 — an error which was repeated by James Joyce in *Ulysses*.

Notes to Narrative

1   William Murray, 1st Earl of Mansfield (1705–93), Chief Justice of the King's Bench, 1756–88; Thomas Erskine, 1st Baron of Restormel (1750–1823), Lord Chancellor, 1806–7; Charles Pratt, 1st Earl Camden (1714–94), Lord Chancellor, 1766–70; Edward Thurlow, 1st Baron (1731–1806), Lord Chancellor, 1778–83.
2   John Lord Somers (1651–1716), Lord Chancellor, 1697–1700; William Pitt, 1st Earl of Chatham (1708–78), Prime Minister, 1766–68; Sir Samuel Romilly (1757–1818), Solicitor General, 1806–7, and law reformer.
3   John Churchill, 1st Duke of Marlborough (1650–1722), victor of Blenheim (1704); Arthur Wellesley, 1st Duke of Wellington (1769–1852), victor of Waterloo (1815) and Prime Minister, 1828–30.
4   Anne (*née* French), Dowager Lady O'Brien (1747–1819), widow of Sir Lucius O'Brien, 3rd Bart.
5   Col. Lucius O'Brien was successfully sued by his servant, whom he had thrashed and seriously injured in a dispute about the latter's wages.
6   On 3 April 1830 Mary Anne Wilton had been delivered of a son in London. On

3 July 1831 she gave birth to a daughter, and both children were baptised at St Margaret's Westminster on 6 January 1832 with the names William and Mary O'Brien, the father being cited as William Smith O'Brien of York Road. Smith O'Brien noted the birth of the son in his day book, paying Mrs Wilton £14, but did not apparently recognise the second child. See Hugh W. L. Weir, 'William Smith O'Brien's Secret Family', *The Other Clare*, xx (1996), pp. 55–6. The terms of the agreement appear not to have been kept.

7   Dr William Griffin, the elder brother of the novelist Gerald Griffin, was a strong political supporter of O'Brien.

8   *Freeman's Journal*, 26, 27 July 1838, considered O'Brien totally wrong to support the final bill commuting tithes into a rent charge, rather than abolishing them.

9   The mistress of Lady O'Brien's father, William Smith.

10   Augustus Stafford O'Brien (in 1847 Stafford-O'Brien) (1811–57) was defeated by his distant relative William Smith O'Brien at the Co. Limerick election of 1837 and petitioned unsuccessfully against the latter's return. He sat as MP for North Northampton from 1841 to 1847.

11   Alderman Joseph Gabbett and his wife Lucy, parents-in-law of William Smith O'Brien.

12   George Howard, Viscount Morpeth and later 7th Earl of Carlisle (1802–64), was popular with Irish MPs when Chief Secretary for Ireland, 1835–41.

13   O'Brien moved on 4 July for a select committee to investigate Irish grievances. Though it failed, he gave a comprehensive indictment of British policy which, published by the Repeal Association, played a part in his decision to join the association later in the year.

14   George Sand, *Consuelo* (Paris, 1843).

15   Lady O'Brien may have been referring to J. P. Molony, originally a Tory, who was struck off the magistracy in 1843 and who identified with Repeal. The family tension was increased by the fact that, shortly before Smith O'Brien's adhesion to Repeal, his brother Sir Lucius had sought signatures for a statement totally repudiating Repeal.

16   Lucy O'Brien's brother, Robert John Gabbett (*c*. 1815–89), then recently graduated from Trinity College, Dublin, and a fellow (tutor) at St Columba's College (Stachallan), before being ordained as a Church of Ireland clergyman and holding a nearby parish.

17   William's sister Catherine, who married Charles Harris, subsequently Bishop of Gibraltar.

18   Agnes Greig, wife of William's great friend from his Cambridge days, Woronzow Greig.

19   O'Brien used Lucy's marriage portion to insure his life with the Sun Life Insurance Company.

20   Probably Rev. Joseph Gabbett, Lucy's brother.

21   The trial of Daniel O'Connell and his chief lieutenants for sedition.

22   Richard was a long-term, reliable servant; Mary seems to have been a maid; Edward, Willie and Lucy were the three children.

23   Lady O'Brien's natural half-sister Jane Brew, *née* Smith, widow of the magistrate Tompkins Brew. Jane Brew supported an imposter, John V. Crosbie, who claimed to be her dead brother Thomas Smith.

24   A controversy had developed over the demand that staff (though not students) at St Columba's College observe Anglican fast days. It led to many resignations, including that of the Warden, the Rev. R. C. Singleton, in June 1846. Edward O'Brien became a student at the college in the same year at the age of nine.

25   O'Brien's sister Anne Martineau was overseeing the deaf child, Willie, at his English school.

26   Father Thomas O'Brien Costelloe (*c*. 1786–1850), PP Murroe, was a leading Repeal organiser in Co. Limerick.

27   Thomas Davis (1814–45), the patriotic journalist of the *Nation*.

28   Alexis Benoit Soyer (1809–58) set up a soup-kitchen in Dublin in 1847 which provided soup at half the usual price.

29   Mamma, Willie, Edward, Lucy, Charlotte, [Robert] Donough (sometimes Don), Lucius, and two servants, Richard and N (or M, Mary).

30   Denis Shine Lawlor (1808–87) of Castlelough, Killarney, was a strong supporter of O'Brien and the Irish Confederation. He was High Sheriff of Kerry in 1840.

31   A reference to the recent transportation of John Mitchel to Bermuda.

32   John Shea Lawlor was a Clare landowner and a strong supporter of O'Brien.

33   The pattern celebrated the martyrdom of St Killian (or Matalogus, or Mokillogue, or Caoinleain) in Würzburg on 8 July 689. He is believed to have sailed from the nearby Bunaw Harbour in 686. John O'Donovan commented on the tussocks in his Ordnance Survey Letters.

34   O'Brien sailed from Glengarriff to Bantry in a yacht owned by the father of Alexander Sullivan, later editor of the *Nation*: 'The instant we rounded the island [Whiddy] there met our view a scene I shall never forget. A flotilla of some hundreds of boats here awaited us. Every crew had gone ashore and pulled green boughs from the trees, and fastened them upright on the gunwales, so that each boat was like a floating bower.' A. M. Sullivan, *New Ireland* (London, 1869), p. 80.

35   Francis Blackburne was soon to preside over O'Brien's own trial for high treason at Clonmel. St Columba's was founded at Stachallan in 1843 by the Rev. William Sewell, who later founded Radley and Glenalmond. Edward was one of the first pupils and wrote a memoir of the school. Smith O'Brien contrasted the treatment of the patriotic clubmen with the schoolboys of the gentry.

36   Woronzow Greig (1805–65), Trinity College, Cambridge, Inner Temple, FRS, barrister on English Northern Circuit.

37   Richard Pennefather (1773–1859), Chief Baron of the Exchequer, 1821–55. His son Richard (1808–49) as High Sheriff of Tipperary organised the trials of Smith O'Brien and his colleagues.

38   Lady O'Brien was wrong. Smith O'Brien attempted an escape from Maria Island on 12 August 1850.

39   Samuel Lapham (1835–76) came to Van Diemen's Land from Kildare. O'Brien left him £500 in his will. O'Brien was accused of behaving improperly with Lapham's daughter Susan. As Susan Wood (1837–80) she became a well-known writer in New Zealand.

40   The Crimean War with Russia broke out two years later.

41   Rev. George Williams (1814–78), a scholar of King's College, Cambridge, and fellow (1835–70), was Warden of St Columba's, 1850–56.

42   Charles Murrough (sometimes Charley) (1849–77) was born when his father was under sentence of death.

43   Though an Anglican, O'Brien sometimes strayed from the church of Archdeacon F. A. Marriott (1811–90) to Catholic (Father W. P. Bond) and Methodist services. Marriott's brother-in-law, William Sharland (1801–77), a surveyor and landowner, also snubbed O'Brien. Sharland's political rival, the Irish Captain Michael Fenton (1789–1874), was very friendly towards O'Brien, as were most other settlers.

44   Joseph and Lucy Gabbett both outlived William Smith O'Brien and Lucy O'Brien, the alderman dying late in 1864 at the age of ninety-two, and his wife in 1867.

45   A condition of the Sun Life Insurance Company was that O'Brien should not go abroad without permission. Permission was refused when O'Brien was transported, and only a small *ex gratia* payment was made. O'Brien's journal was first published, as *'To Solitude Consigned'*, by the Crossing Press of Sydney in 1995.

46   The report was false, as O'Brien had turned down an opportunity to escape.

47   Patrick J. Smyth (1826–85) was a Young Irelander sent to Van Diemen's Land by the New York Irish Directory to organise O'Brien's escape, but the latter insisted that Mitchel go instead. Smyth later sat in parliament for Westmeath and Tipperary. Mitchel, on his escape, caused an outcry from United States abolitionists like Harriet Beecher Stowe, author of *Uncle Tom's Cabin*, by vehemently supporting slavery.

48   The deaf son Willie was sent to a special school in England and often stayed with his aunt, Anne Martineau, who lived at Whitkirk Vicarage, Yorkshire, 1838–63, with her husband, the Rev. Arthur Martineau (1807–72).

49   The end of the letter gives the correct location of this disaster. On 21 January 1854 the *Tayleur*, an iron clipper-ship, with 579 from Liverpool bound for Melbourne,

struck a rock on the east of Lambay Island, sinking immediately. Only 280 were saved, according to the *Nation*, 28 Jan. 1854.

50   Williams was accused of treating the son of Chief Justice Francis Blackburne too leniently. The boys refused to end a boycott and were supported by their parents. Archbishop J. C. Beresford was also concerned that Williams associated with members of the Oxford Movement. See G. K. White, *A History of St Columba's College, 1843–1974* (Dublin, 1980). pp. 63, 65.

51   Sir Lucius O'Brien's first wife Mary, *née* Fitzgerald of Adelphi, died in 1852. Lucius in 1854 married Louisa Finucane, twenty-one years younger. See Letter 34 for Lucy's positive reaction to the new Lady O'Brien.

52   William's brother Robert married Elinor de Vere, sister of the poet Aubrey de Vere. The family had converted to Catholicism.

53   William Monsell (later Lord Emly) was elected alongside Smith O'Brien as MP for Co. Limerick in 1847. Like the de Veres, he was converted to Catholicism. His brother, the Rev. Charles Monsell, married O'Brien's sister Harriet.

54   An attempt by Charles Gavan Duffy and others to set up an independent Irish party in the House of Commons foundered when its leading members, William Keogh and John Sadleir, defected in late 1852 to take government office.

55   Egg-laying mammal, duck-billed platypus.

56   O'Brien's efforts to send a kangaroo rat, and possibly a platypus (ornithorhyncus), home to his children were unsuccessful.

57   O'Brien did not reach Sydney, but attended a reception in Melbourne.

58   Husband of William's sister Catherine (Kate).

59   'My lot in its beginnings was restless, and I am weary of my toils undertaken without an end and without honour.' Ovid, *Metamorphoses*, II, 386–7.

60   'I wrap myself in my virtue, and seek virtuous poverty without a dowry.' Horace, *Odes*, III, xxix, 56.

61   This may have been a serious throat infection that struck half the boys and killed two. Though medical opinion indicated that the school authorities were not at fault, numbers dropped from 60 to 40. Gwynn took a northern benefice in 1864.

62   Probably Edward Twells (1828–98), the first Bishop of the Orange Free State, 1863–70.

Bibliography

Manuscripts

William Smith O'Brien Papers (National Library of Ireland)
Inchiquin Papers (National Library of Ireland)
Anthony O'Brien Papers (in private ownership)
Robin Gwynn Papers (in private ownership)

Sources of individual documents

1. William Smith O'Brien Papers, MS 426, no. 1
2. Ibid., MS 8655 (3)
3. Ibid.
4. Inchiquin Papers, MS 3627
5. Ibid., MS 3034
6. William Smith O'Brien Papers, MS 428, no. 291
7. Ibid., MS 8656 (4)
8. Ibid.
9. Ibid., MS 8653 (5)
10. Ibid., MS 8653 (13)
11. Anthony O'Brien Papers
12. William Smith O'Brien Papers, MS 431, no. 801
13. Ibid., MS 8653 (17)
14. Ibid., MS 433, no. 1071
15. Ibid., MS 433, no. 1093
16. Ibid., MS 8654 (2)
17. Ibid., MS 8654 (7)
18. Ibid., MS 8653 (20)
19. Inchiquin Papers, MS 3757
20. Ibid.
21. William Smith O'Brien Papers, MS 8654 (7)
22. Ibid., MS 436, no. 1569
23. Ibid., MS 8654 (7)
24. Ibid., MS 438, no. 1816
25. Ibid., MS 8653 (24)
26. Ibid.
27. Ibid., MS 8655 (12)
28. Ibid., MS 8655 (10)

29.   Ibid., MS 444, no. 2726
30.   Ibid., MS 8653 (28)
31.   Ibid.
32.   Ibid., MS 8654 (6)
33.   Ibid., MS 8653 (30)
34.   Ibid., MS 8654 (10)
35.   Robin Gwynn Papers, 13 (1)
36.   William Smith O'Brien Papers, MS 8654 (4)
37.   Anthony O'Brien Papers, Journal of an Excursion made during the months of August and September 1861 by William Smith O'Brien, p. 1.
38.   Robin Gwynn Papers
39.   William Smith O'Brien Papers, MS 8663, Misc. Papers
40.   Anthony O'Brien Papers

Newspapers

Freeman's Journal, Dublin
Nation, Dublin

Printed Books

Davis, Richard, *The Young Ireland Movement* (Dublin & New Jersey, 1987)
—— *William Smith O'Brien: Ireland — 1848 — Tasmania* (Dublin, 1989)
—— 'William Smith O'Brien and the American Civil War' in *Canadian Journal of Irish Studies*, xix, no. 2 (1993), pp. 45–53
—— 'William Smith O'Brien as an Imperialist' in Rebecca Pelan (ed.), *Irish-Australian Studies: Papers delivered at the Seventh Irish-Australian Conference, July 1993* (Sydney, 1994), pp. 8–242
—— *William Smith O'Brien: Ticket-of-Leave, New Norfolk* (Hobart, 1996)
—— 'William Smith O'Brien and Tasmanian Convict Workers' in Barry Dyster (ed.), *Beyond Convict Workers* (Sydney, 1996), pp. 54–63
—— *et al.* (eds), *'To Solitude Consigned': The Tasmanian Journal of William Smith O'Brien, 1849–53* (Sydney, 1995)
de Vere, Aubrey, *Recollections* (London, 1897)
Gwynn, Denis, *Young Ireland and 1848* (Cork, 1948)
Gwynn, Stephen, *Charlotte Grace O'Brien* (Dublin, 1909)
—— *Experiences of a Literary Man* (London, 1926)
O'Brien, Grania, *These My Friends and Forebears: The O'Briens of Dromoland* (Whitegate, Co. Clare, 1991)

O'Brien, Ivar, *O'Brien of Thomond: The O'Briens in Irish History, 1500–1865* (Chichester, 1986)

Sullivan, A. M., *New Ireland* (London, 1878)

Venn, J. A. (ed.), *Alumni Cantabrigienses, Part II: 1752–1900* (Cambridge, 1947)

Weir, Hugh W. L., 'William Smith O'Brien's Secret Family', *The Other Clare*, xx (1996), pp. 55–6

White, G. K., *A History of St Columba's College, 1843–1974* (Dublin, 1980)

Index